SUSTAINABLE IN STILETTOS

A style-conscious guide to navigating
the evolving world of fashion and beyond...

Tracey L. Martin

emerge
publishing

TULSA, OKLAHOMA

22 21 20 19 18 17   8 7 6 5 4 3 2 1

SUSTAINABLE IN STILETTOS — A style-conscious guide to navigating the evolving world of fashion and beyond

Published by:

TULSA, OKLAHOMA

Emerge Publishing, LLC
9521B Riverside Parkway, Suite 243
Tulsa, Oklahoma 74137
Phone: 888.407.4447
www.EmergePublishing.com

Author website: www.sustainableinstilettos.com

Library of Congress Cataloging-in-Publication Data
ISBN: 978-1-943127-77-1 Paperback
ISBN: 978-1-943127-78-8 Digital/E-book

BISAC Category:
BUS070090 BUSINESS & ECONOMICS / Industries / Fashion & Textile Industry
BUS072000 BUSINESS & ECONOMICS / Development / Sustainable Development
BUS099000 BUSINESS & ECONOMICS / Environmental Economics

Printed in the United States

TABLE OF CONTENTS

ABOUT THE COVER IMAGE...

Can you recall the feeling you got when a new album or CD came out, and you couldn't wait to read all about the cover art and to see what the artist had created? I feel the same way about book cover art. I often wonder why the author chose a certain color or graphic and was there a story behind it. The cover tells a story even before you open the book. We hope you enjoy ours.

This cover was first conceptualized in my head in the middle of the night (when most creative things come to me). I saw it, and then I had to bring it to life. However, I knew it would have to be special, and I knew I needed some badass women to assist me in making it come to life!

The message in the dress...

There are so many messages within this dress. First of all the fabric. Sustainable organic hemp silk. Gorgeous hand feel that is good for the wearer, and the earth. It has a subtle sheen and beautiful character. I chose to use natural indigo dye. It's synthetic alter ego is one of the most toxic dyes on the planet. I wanted to bring awareness to the current state of our waterways around the world due to the synthetic form of this color. The vision for the dress was to be a vintage denim piece. I think we nailed it! The dress had to be versatile. As in life, things are always changing and rearranging. The overlay shredded skirt is detachable and reveals a simple ombre dyed halter gown underneath. The overlay skirt is made up of shredded pieces that are torn and sewn together to signify that each one of us individually is vital to the creation as a whole. Such is life. Life is art.

"It really does take a village!"

Jeanne Hankerson. You will read more about her in the sustainable wedding paragraphs in the book. This would not have happened without her—that I know for sure. Jeanne was so excited when I shared my vision with her that it was almost palatable. I told her that we needed to design and build a dress in layers. Because I believe that we only evolve into the best version of ourselves when we allow life to add layers to who we are so we can become who we are meant to be. Those layers had to be torn instead of cut to represent the "rough edges" that we all have. The rawness of being vulnerable had to be represented. This was accomplished when Jeanne sat in her studio one Saturday afternoon and ripped and tore pieces of delicious natural fabrics into strips. Once they were torn, she set about measuring each strip and putting them in piles so that our seamstress could attach them in just the right way. The waist band was carefully measured so that it would fit perfectly. The base of the dress is a beautiful organic hemp silk wedding dress that Jeanne had previously designed for her wedding collection.

Who would be the cover model? I thought about it and realized that everyone who would be working on the dress and the cover, came from all over the USA and were from all walks of life, all ages, and generations. So I needed to keep that theme. Who else to model this but my beautiful youngest daughter, Marina Martin. This completed the generational circle. My girls represent every reason for why I do what I do.

We went to Jeanne's studio and discussed the details. We wanted to create the dress locally. So we contacted FABRIC building in Tempe. They were ready to jump on board and provide us a with a beautiful place to work for an afternoon. Bianca Sanford, one of their very talented interns, took on the task of sewing the overlay piece and assembling the creation. Even offering to take the dress home to ensure that it was completed on time. Of course, timing is always of the essence so when we received the phone call that it was completed, we headed down to see the progress. We were so pleased with the work they had done. When talented people come together for a cause, anything can be accomplished!

I picked up this gorgeous dress and headed to LA to my dye house to have the dress dipped in our natural plant based indigo dyes. Our first hurdle! Ugh. The dye house said that their machines were too aggressive on agitating and would destroy our creation. The dress would have to be dyed entirely by hand. WOW, this truly was a sustainable collaboration of multi layers! Plan B for dyeing. I then contacted the brilliant Dr. Sherry Haar at Kansas State University Dept. of Apparel and Textiles. I was familiar with Sherry's work. The only thing I wasn't certain about was the timing. I took a chance and explained the entire process to her and the vision. Sherry jumped on board

3

and would lend her talent to ensure this dress was the perfect indigo blue!

Once the dress was on its way to Sherry, I have to admit that I did breathe a little easier. Sherry is a brilliant natural dyer, and I knew the dress was in good hands. Words can't describe the feeling I had once I saw this part of the dress come to life. Sherry sent images of the dress throughout the process. Those of you that know me know that I was dying (no pun intended) inside not to be there in person. But Sherry kept the images coming! The dress is truly a work of art that had been touched by so many talented women and their artisan's hands. Sherry used De La Terre Colours GOTS certified organic plant based dye.

Oh, for someone to create the perfect ethereal makeup look. I need look no further than the multi-talented Daniela La-Farga. She showed up at my house bright and early and put her talents to work.

For the photographer, what can I say? I would not settle for anyone other than the extraordinary photographer, Kelly Cappelli. She is a force in the world of creatives. A talented painter, photographer and all around stellar human! Her talent is off the charts, and her vision is brighter than anyone I know! Things always seem to be magical when we work together. She was accompanied by her amazing assistant Nichole Town.

MORE THAN A BOOK COVER

The dress will be entered into a few "green" dress competitions and will eventually be auctioned off with the proceeds going to a charity of our choice or a scholarship for one lucky fashion student studying sustainability! Follow the journey on our Instagram for all the latest updates **@sustainableinstilettos**

My hope is that our readers will come to look forward to our beautiful covers on all of our soon to be released books with the same anticipation that I had every time my favorite band would release an album or CD. I couldn't wait to see the design and read the story behind it.

Thank you to everyone who had a "hand" in this creation.

My heart is so full as I hold this book in my hands knowing who has been a part of this beautiful cover. I am so blessed to have so many talented and selfless people who are willing to be a part of this journey.

Special & humbled Thanks to:

Jeanne Hankerson - fellow collaborator, designer and beautiful soul

Kelly Cappelli - photographer and very special human

Bianca Sansford - seamstress and one talented soul

Marina Martin - model and amazing daughter of mine.

Daniel Lafarga - Makeup, hair and all around badass

Sherry Haar - natural textile dye extraordinaire, responsible for the gorgeous colors of the dress.

Sherri Barry - FABRIC Tempe providing a place to work

Risa Kostis - For letting me borrow the perfect pair of red shoes. I wouldn't settle for anything else.

Emily Andrews - Sherry Haar's patient and diligent dye assistant. Emily is an undergraduate student at K-State.

DEDICATION

I dedicate this book to a very special man in my life, Chad Mooney. Chad has been battling Stage 4 colon cancer for the past four years. He has taught me that every day is a gift and that we are not guaranteed tomorrow. Do your work, show up and be kind. Go after what you want. Even if something is difficult, do it with dignity. Be of service to others and if you can help someone, do it! "Every day is a gift." Thank you, Chad, you are irreplaceable!

A heartfelt thank you to my wonderful family,

Tommy my soulmate my rock and my 2 beautiful daughters and muses, Mekenna and Marina for being patient and understanding while I spent countless hours locked away in my office or the library. You are my everything. I will work tirelessly to do my part in leaving you a better world. I love you all more than all the grains of sand in the ocean a million times.

To my parents, thank you for the unconditional love, support and unwavering example of grace throughout my life. I love you more than words can express.

Matt Gould - Thank you for your love and support on many levels.

A special thank you to Kim Stredney for her editorial assistance.

MY WHY!

Why am I so passionate about sustainable fashion? So driven to be a part of the change we need to see in this industry and the world? So vehement about sustainable living as a lifestyle? It is because I know this is the only way humanity, our environment, and the animal kingdom can survive and thrive.

Growing up in the Midwest, my childhood was about as close to perfect as possible. Although to me, it was just the way the world was...or so I thought. I felt happy and free running through beautiful fields and alongside rushing creeks and spending time with family filled up my days. Memories of watching the leaves change in the fall, snowball fights in the winter and catching and releasing lightning bugs in the summer continue to play back in my mind as an adult.

Waking up every morning to breakfast made from organic fruits and vegetables from our home garden and riding my horse to the treehouse to play on the tire swing was how every normal kid spent their time, right? For my family, it was all about the simple things. Friday night horse shows and weekend camping trips were just a natural part of life. Ice skating on our frozen pond and coming home from school to a new litter of puppies jumping all over me was just the way it was in my wonderful little world.

Respect for humans, animals and the earth is in the fabric of my DNA. I was taught to care for animals the same way I would care for a friend or family member. And our food was something we grew ourselves and took pride in cultivating. My mom had dinner on the table every night when we came home from one of our many school activities, whether it was cheerleading, soccer, softball or volleyball. I'm not sure if I took it for granted, but it was always a given that this is how our family did things. Buying vegetables, fruits, meats, and treats in stores was hardly ever done in our house. My mom canned veggies and fruits in the summer so we had delectable delicacies to look forward to eating in the winter. We did raise a few cows, and we would butcher one a year. Yes, one cow fed my family for an entire YEAR! Nothing was wasted. (This was, of course, before I adopted a more vegan-principled lifestyle.)

The true value of things was talked about a lot in our home; not just the "cost" of something, but the significance it held as well. I was lucky to be able to go to work with my Dad on the weekends so I could learn the value of hard work. Because of this, I grew up with a strong work ethic and was grateful for everything. We were taught that our clothing had to last, and we had to take care of them. Back to school shopping meant we would each get two pairs of jeans, a few cute tops and one pair of shoes. One year, my Mom hired a seamstress to make some of our clothing for us, and I was bitten by the fashion bug. I still remember to this day how much fun we had going through patterns and picking out our own fabrics. To think I could create a piece of clothing no one else would own was pretty cool to me, so developing my own sense of style started early. My mom was very understanding when I would walk down stairs with a pair of scissors, a pair of jeans, and maybe a bottle of bleach. Or some cranberry juice and a white tee shirt. She would just look at me, smile and shake her head.

Fast forward to today, and that life seems like a long-gone, Mayberry-type existence. My gratitude to my parents for raising me this way, however, is immeasurable. It doesn't escape me that not everyone can grow up with this experience. However, we can all do better with what we do have. Every single day, I work to instill the same values and ideals I was raised on in my own two daughters—to teach them the value of their food, clothing, and home. My girls are online homeschooled, so they are exposed to "real" life skills that they need. Their education isn't limited to what can be taught within the confines of four walls. We teach them banking skills, how to budget, how to cook, and the value of their health, and honoring their overall wellness. They enjoy the freedom to experience many things other children who are at school all day might not have the opportunity to do. My girls travel with me to see fashion designers, authors, speakers, manufacturers, dye houses and warehouses, and have met some pretty fantastic humans! This life choice still has its challenges, but we can overcome those as well.

My passion runs deep for this industry and the impact it is having on our planet, animals, and humanity as a whole. We must learn to buy less and buy better, not in a self-depriving way, but in a way that feeds our souls on every level. It is not about giving something up; it is about gaining so much more! A beautiful, sustainable lifestyle can offer pure fulfillment to every inch of the mind-body-spirit connection.

> *"Creating a more sustainable life is not about depriving yourself. It is about creating abundance through better choices. It is not about self-depriving, it is about abundantly thriving." — Tracey Martin*

When we think of our legacy and what our children and younger generations to come are going to be left with, we need to look at the state of the world today. How we treat this planet and all its living beings is a direct reflection of who we are today. And the statistics on the current state of the planet are mind-boggling:

Over 150 billion farmed animals are slaughtered every year by humans, and the manner in which they are killed is an atrocity.[1]

---

1   http://www.adaptt.org/

We use 1,800 gallons of water to grow the cotton, which is then spun into yarn, made into fabric, dyed, and sewn together to make one pair of jeans; and some of us own 20 or more pairs at any given time![2]

Fruits and vegetables grown around the world that don't meet certain aesthetic standards are wastefully tossed out.[3] While millions of people are going hungry!

I believe because this country has been blessed with so many resources and so much opportunity, we have never had to develop the discipline to conserve and nurture this world. If this principle was **not** taught to you in your home, where would you learn it? We eat too much food in general, consuming massive amounts of meat, sugar and processed foods. We consume clothing like it was made to be disposable and just thrown away. We treat animals as if they are a commodity for our gluttonous pleasure without realizing they are living beings with brains, souls, and feelings. We clearly have misused our power. How much longer do we really think this can continue?

Ask yourself this, and make it personal, "What is my threshold for pain before I am willing to change?" When your doctor says you are a few cheeseburgers away from a heart attack, you are emotionally moved to make better choices because you see your own mortality directly in front of you. Red meat consumption is on a decline today—but not because we are

---

2   http://wateruseitwisely.com/it-takes-1800-gallons-of-water-to-make-one-pair-of-jeans/

3   https://www.theguardian.com/environment/2016/jul/13/us-food-waste-ugly-fruit-vegetables-perfect
     https://thinkprogress.org/selling-ugly-fruits-and-vegetables-could-be-key-to-solving-americas-food-waste-problem-57734f3b5bba/

caring more about the animals or the environment. It is be-cause we are starting to wake up to how it affects our health and the amount of chemicals and hormones that are used. We tend to make changes only when something affects us person-ally. Human beings are selfish like that.

Our collective behavior of consumerism and consumption is at an all-time high, and our levels of happiness, wellness, and prosperity are at an all-time low. Our environment is suffering, and our ecosystems are broken. Things aren't adding up, and it's time we change our viewpoint. True joy is an inside job, and it begins within the self. I am starting with me. I have heard and responded to my own inner call to action. I will show up for it 100 percent. My only question is: **Will you join me?**

SUSTAINABLE IN STILETTOS

"**A** style-conscious guide to navigating the evolving world of fashion and beyond."

When one pulls at a single thing in nature one finds it attached to everything else." –John Muir

We, as a species, are slowly waking up to the ecological and ethical ramifications of how our collective actions have affected every aspect of life on this planet. Most recently, the onset of books like *The Third Plate* by Dan Barber, *Skinny Bitch* by Rory Freedman and Kim Barnouim and *The China Study* by T. Colin Campbell, Ph.D., and Thomas Campbell, M.D., as well as documentaries such as *Forks Over Knives, Earthling,* and *Cowspiracy,* have opened our eyes to the overwhelming and hard-to-swallow *truths* behind the farming and meat processing industries.

Truths such as:

Millions of male chicks are ground alive by a large machine[4] because they cannot produce eggs, so there is no use for them.

---

4 http://www.independent.co.uk/life-style/food-and-drink/hatched-discarded-gassed-what-happens-to-male-chicks-in-the-uk-10088509.html

Most of the antibiotics produced in the world are injected directly into the meat you eat, bringing about drug-resistant bacteria.[5]

Many chickens are butchered in the U.S., shipped to China for processing[6] (getting pumped full of plumping agents and color in the process) and then sent back to the U.S. for distribution in our local grocery stores.

The onslaught of food labels hitting the grocery store shelves has also been both educational and at the same time, puzzling:

GMO, Non-GMO, Gluten-Free, Organic, Natural, Grass-Fed, Free Range, Antibiotics, rBST-Free... Wait, WHAT?!

I just want to feed my family healthy, nourishing food. Even when it comes to the farming of our foods, that process is no longer the same as it has been for hundreds of years. There are so many chemicals used in farming today, and we are being experimented on and lied too—sometimes intentionally, sometimes not. The farmers may not even be fully informed. Crops are no longer rotated to regenerate the soil. Seeds have all been modified, and the water used for irrigation is contaminated and leeches into our soil and food sources. I think it's safe to say we are completely dazed and confused.

Little by little though, we are slowly beginning to do our homework and decipher what all of these new terms mean. We still have work to do, but many of us have arrived at a place where we are finally able to make smart, ecologically sound nu-

5   https://www.peta.org/living/food/meat-contamination/
     http://www.pbs.org/wgbh/pages/frontline/shows/meat/safe/overview.
     html
6   http://www.newsweek.com/2014/10/10/curious-case-chinese-chicken-
     import-export-business-273699.html

trition decisions for ourselves and our families. We are more aware of the fact that food is our medicine and that our daily habits affect people all over the world. We are aware that there are chemicals we need to look out for in our personal products, skincare, and makeup. As well as the fact that we are living amongst some of the most toxic chemicals every day in our homes.

Now it is time to turn our attention to our clothing in our closets, the fashion industry, and our daily buying habits and the rate at which we are consuming.

The mission of this book is to bridge the gap between the mystery and myths surrounding the fashion industry and the educated customer—that's you! I want you to ask questions. I want you to be emotionally moved to create change. I want to disrupt your daily thoughts and habits. To help you redefine what your true style is.

My goal is to shed light on the harmful practices that take place daily within this industry and to better define some of the language found in brand messaging and on clothing labels. You, as the conscious consumer, are part of the market research that is required for the industry to realize that change is needed so that its leaders will make the necessary ethical choices for the environment, animals, and people.

In this book, I want to spotlight the wonderful organizations walking the talk and providing an open door for all of us to enter through. We can all be disruptors in our daily buying habits, and therefore, within the industry.

We, as consumers, have the power to demand change by making conscious decisions on how, when, and where we spend our money. Think of each item of clothing or food you buy as a vote you are casting in favor of that specific brand, its ethics, and its practices. When you purchase from companies that are not operating under ethical business practices, you are in a sense giving them permission to continue their corrupt, "business-as-usual" ways. The number of consumers by far outweighs the number of brands; therefore, sustainability is our collective and ultimate responsibility. It is time we start using our voices and dollars to let labels know what we will and what we won't stand for in fashion, food, beauty, home, and every aspect of our daily lives.

Is it possible to look good and do good? YES! But first, we must find solutions, connect influencers and collaborate with one another to enact real change for the betterment of us all.

We must collectively address the global concerns that are all around us—from the conversations on global warming to what we eat, wear, drive, and our homes. Each one of these entities are threads in our lives that are intricately woven together to make us WHO we are and HOW we live. As a whole, consumers are becoming more sophisticated in their buying habits. It is an awakening to how we impact our world.

There is a better way to live our lives today. A more fulfilling, beautiful and mindful way! Each one of us can choose to show up differently in this world. Humanity will be the largest benefactor of our actions. Choose a more peaceful life through your choices.

In this book, I have included a chapter on definitions of terms that you will find in your daily life as you begin to wake up to a more sustainable way of living. You will see these terms on labels, on websites, and in articles that you read. Be informed so you can make the best decisions for you, your family, and the future of the planet.

As a bonus, I have included a massive resource-sustainable shopping guide. I have listed brands that you can learn about and support. Chapter 9 is chocked full of great websites to visit so that you can be in the know. Then in chapter 10, there are influencers you can follow, books to read, and documentaries to watch so that you can become a student of sustainable living.

Let me just put this out there. According to the first joint report from McKinsey Global Fashion Index and the Business of Fashion, the fashion industry generated about $2.4 trillion dollars last year. In fact, not only does fashion touch every one of us but it would be the world's seventh largest economy if ranged alongside the GDP of individual countries.[7]

Disclaimer: *I absolutely LOVE fashion. I love the story it tells. I love the creative minds behind the designs, and I love the fabulous textures and colors. This is why I am so passionate about creating positive change within the industry! We must praise the move in the right direction no matter how small.*

---

7   http://www.mckinsey.com/industries/retail/our-insights/the-state-of-fashion

Chapter 1

The Ugly Side of a Beautiful Industry

WARNING: REALITY CHECK UP AHEAD!

I truly believe at this moment in time the fashion industry itself is the number one obstacle standing in the way of creating lasting change for all those touched by the industry. This is purely because the people who are running it continue to choose massive profits over the welfare of people, animals, and our planet—time and time again.

The onset of fast fashion[8] in the past 20-plus years has brought with it a whole host of residual effects. However, this is not the only factor that has propelled us to reach our current breaking point. High-end designers, mega-brands, and the consumers who purchase these products must also assume their

8   http://www.greenpeace.org/international/en/news/Blogs/makingwaves/
     fast-fashion-drowning-world-fashion-revolution/blog/56222/
     http://news.trust.org//item/20150224161518-w5ipm/

fair share of responsibility for this broken system that is causing Mother Earth and humanity to pay the ultimate price. And, as global citizens, we can't turn a blind eye. First, we must realize we ALL have had a hand in this—myself included! If you have ever purchased or worn an item of clothing, you have been a willing, albeit perhaps unaware (up until now), participant in this downward spiral.

From this point forward, you have ZERO excuse to say, "I had no idea this was happening!"

Historically, fashion designers made four or five seasonal collections per year and followed an organized business model in releasing each collection. But that model was long ago abandoned and replaced with a system that is less sustainable. Today, some mega fashion brands release upward of 42 collections within a 12-month period! Can you imagine the amount of planning, resources, and labor that must go into pulling off an operation like that? Yes, this is providing jobs, but at what cost?

I walked into Forever 21 the other day to have a look around and do my own investigation. I spoke with one of the salespeople, and she informed me that they get shipments of new designs in almost *daily*. The insatiable appetite of the consumer is out of control. We are behaving like spoiled brats at the candy shop, grabbing everything in sight with no regard for the repercussions our gluttony will inevitably cause.

It is a hard fact that we are using up nature's resources at a rate we can't possibly replace—and all for the sake of our next Friday night outfit! Oh, the horror if we are seen in the same outfit twice! Funny, I always thought our clothes were meant to work for us, not just to be worn once and hung in our closets like ornaments, or worse...thrown out! There seems to be a common theme of disposable behavior running through all aspects of our lives—from the clothing we wear to the food we consume and even the family, friendships, and romantic relationships we engage in. We have forgotten the cardinal rule that to make something last, we need to truly invest in it, nurture it, and be intentional in our actions.

What would you gain if you simplified your life and were content with what you currently have?

Human beings are destroying landscapes, cultures, and ecosystems for the sake of fashion and profit. In the U.S., 97% of all apparel sold is made outside of the country, and the residents of some of these locations are paying the ultimate price to manufacture *our* clothing. Life expectancy for some is cut short due to toxic chemical use, and families are experiencing alarming rates of birth defects, cancer, and other deadly diseases because they live in or near high manufacturing areas and are exposed daily to these hazards. It is a slow death.

According to recent UN reports, pesticides are responsible for 200,000 acute poisoning deaths each year, and chronic exposure is linked to cancer, Alzheimer's, Parkinson's disease, hormone disruption, development disorders, and sterility.[9]

---

9   http://articles.mercola.com/sites/articles/archive/2017/08/01/chemical-biotechnology-threatens-environmental-human-health.aspx

Chemicals and dyes are being dumped into rivers, lakes, and oceans by companies[10] who have no qualms whatsoever about damaging our delicate ecosystem just to make a buck.

Workers are living on less than a dollar a day but are begging for more and even forming unions to have their voices heard. These women and children are promised opportunities, only to find out that they have instead become slaves. Women are leaving their children behind so they can go to work in factories hundreds of miles away from their villages, hopeful to bring home money to make life better for their families—sometimes not seeing their children more than twice a year. Tragically, some of these women never make it home, or if they do, they have suffered horrible accidents and sustained life-altering physical damage.

These atrocities happen every single day in factories and manufacturing facilities, all around the world. But media coverage brought attention to one such tragic event that happened in 2013 at Rana Plaza in Bangladesh. When the Savar factory (a building that housed subcontractors working for major global fashion brands) collapsed in 2013, more than 1,100 women, children, and men were killed, and 2,500 more were injured.[11] This tragedy is considered to be the deadliest accident in the fashion industry in modern history, but what is impossible to grasp is that it didn't have to happen. All the cracks and damage to the facility were brought to the attention of the owners,

10 http://www.greenpeace.org/usa/fashion-brands-including-gap-brooks-brothers-dumping-toxic-wastewater-in-indonesia-waterways/
    http://www.environmentamerica.org/news/ame/206-million-pounds-toxic-chemicals-dumped-america%E2%80%99s-waterways
11 https://en.wikipedia.org/wiki/2013_Savar_building_collapse

who chose to look the other way. The lower level of the building housed a bank and numerous shops that were closed after the structural issues were found, but the garment workers were ordered to continue working on the upper floors. Most likely, this was due to pressure from the factory owners and management, as well as the buyers and agents working for the brands to complete orders on time so they could protect their bottom line. I don't know about you, but there is nothing in my closet that is worth a life!

WHO ARE WE? ARE TODAY'S CONSUMERS MORE NARCISSISTIC AND HEARTLESS THAN EVER?

We are a narcissistic, self-centered society;[12] and yet, we have no "SENSE OF SELF"—no sense whatsoever of who we are or what we stand for. Yes, we are all consumers, in the broadest sense of the word. Why do we choose to listen to the media, advertisers, and marketers rather than doing our own research? Why do we participate in the game of buying more, more and more stuff that we clearly do not need? The very term "consumer" drives me crazy. It evokes thoughts of humans running around like little Pac-men greedily eating up everything just to fulfill their own selfish needs and wants. I am not speaking of basic needs. I am talking about everything above that line. So, from now on, let's use the term **customer** instead.

We, as customers, have truly lost our collective minds when it comes to shopping and consuming. I believe excessive want is our way of filling a void in another area of our lives. Shopping

12   http://www.abc.net.au/radionational/programs/allinthemind/young-people-today-are-more-narcissistic-than-ever/5457236

is an addiction for many. We have clothes in our closets with tags still on them, never worn. We buy more than we can afford and more than we need. We scour Instagram to see what "everyone" else has, and we believe that we need it too.

Learn to tell yourself NO to material things you don't need! I, too, love to shop and enjoy all the beautiful things that are available. However, there comes a time when we need to set our compass right and really think about why we purchase and what we purchase.

> *"Choosing to live more sustainably is the highest form of spirituality. It means we realize we are all connected, and we all share this world and all that it offers. It is abundant thinking instead of closed-minded consumerism" — Tracey Martin*

Have we become so far removed from the rest of the world that we don't even give a passing thought as to who is providing us with the clothing we wear? We need to remember that there is a human face and a pair of hands behind every single article of clothing, piece of jewelry, pair of shoes, and handbag we own. Next time you set out on a shopping trip, ask yourself these questions first:

Who made this piece of clothing?
What is that person's life like?
How many times will I really wear this?
How much will I use this?

Where will it go when I no longer want it?

**"If anything matters, then everything matters."
–Tracey Martin**

<u>Fast Fact:</u> **Cotton is the world's most important non-food agricultural commodity, and India is home to over one-third of the world's cotton farmers.**

Recently, alarming facts have come to light regarding cotton farmers in India and the agreements they entered into with large corporations. After signing a contract with these companies that many of them didn't even fully understand, farmers in an area known as the "Cotton Belt" were supplied with seeds to grow BT cotton, a genetically modified organism that was introduced to the world in 2002. The farmers were told that this type of cotton would be resistant to insects, meaning they wouldn't have to purchase expensive herbicides and pesticides to protect their crops. Unfortunately, these "pest-resistant" crops only lasted a little while—their resistance soon faded. [13]

Think about this, many people take antibiotics prescribed by their doctor, and we also ingest them in the foods we eat. Eventually though, because of such mass exposure, we build up a resistance to them. This same effect is what happened to the cotton crop in India, leaving the farmers no option but to purchase the herbicides and pesticides to save what little crops they had left. The farmers were not educated on these chem-

---

13 http://seedfreedom.info/monsanto-illegally-introduces-round-up-resistant-gmo-cotton-in-india/

icals nor their potential for toxicity in the environment and to humankind.

<u>Fast Fact:</u> **The chemical, glyphosate,[14] which is the active ingredient in Roundup has been listed as a known carcinogen under California's Proposition 65. This means it will need to carry a cancer causing warning label.**

Due to the dwindling harvest and high cost of seeds and herbicides, the farmers found themselves deep in a cycle of debt, and quite often, bankruptcy. [15] When they signed the agreements to purchase the seeds, most of them did not have enough money to buy the amount they would need, so they either put up their land as collateral or took out loans, often at an interest rate of 40 percent. When the crops do not produce as promised, the farmers don't have enough profits to pay back their seed loans, so the corporation takes their land as payment.

<u>Fast Fact:</u> **700 million people (roughly 60% of the Indian population) are directly or indirectly dependent upon agriculture for survival.[16] The second largest group (10–12 million people) are dependent upon the textile industry.**

What was once a holistic, sustainable, diversified agricultural system has been replaced with an unsustainable globalized

---

14   http://archive.lankabusinessonline.com/news/sri-lanka-killer-kidney-disease-linked-to-monsanto-weedicide,-phosphate-fertilizer:-study/2081217214
     https://www.ncbi.nlm.nih.gov/pubmed/22331240
15   http://www.globalresearch.ca/the-seeds-of-suicide-how-monsanto-destroys-farming/5329947
     http://www.law.nyu.edu/news/chrgj_report_every_thirty_minutes_india
16   http://www.worldwatch.org/asia-and-africa-home-95-percent-global-agricultural-population

agribusiness controlled by the greed and power of corrupt corporations. These biotech companies are not only financially
wealthy; they also have powerful lobbyists in Congress looking
out for their interests instead of the interests of the people and
our precious environment and resources.

WHAT MORE CAN BE DONE?

I personally believe there need to be programs implemented
by these large global corporations to educate and assist farmers in creating a sustainable business. As soon as we wake up
and realize that farmers are truly the backbone of some of the
most important industries on this planet, we will finally start
to value them and begin putting the programs in place to assist them in building thriving businesses and putting safety and
health programs in place to create change.

Fast Fact: **"99% of the world's cotton farmers live and
work in the developing world."[17]**

It's no secret that clothing brands deliberately source from
and manufacture their products in economically challenged
countries because they know they will be dealing with inad-
equate labor laws poorly regulated by the factories. Illiteracy
is often rampant, so labeling of any kind bearing warnings for
worker safety goes mostly unread. Health and safety regulations are virtually non-existent in many of these places, so it is
much cheaper to do business there. Bad business behavior is
what landed us in this mess. It would seem logical then that in
order to not recreate this situation, we must find a way to raise

17 https://ejfoundation.org/resources/downloads/the_deadly_chemicals_
    in_cotton.pdf

the level of integrity and consciousness of the capitalist that exist today. There are billions and billions of transactions taking place every day in the marketplaces all around the world. Can there ever be enough regulations in place or laws passed? Or do we need to look at this differently? Do we need to make it personal? Do we need to behave differently? Do we need to take more responsibility for our actions? Has anyone taken the true cost into consideration for workers, their families, and our future world?

"Every crisis is an opportunity to create change." — Tracey Martin

Some large brands have started to use only "approved" factories, but this opens the door for another large loophole. When the so-called approved factories can no longer handle the workload, they often subcontract out to another local third-party factory that is not regulated or monitored. When this happens and undercover agents expose it, these companies respond with a heartfelt excuse such as, "We had NO idea about this!" The problem is, if it happened once, it will happen again.

Fast Fact: **There are millions of people enslaved today, more than in any other time in history.**[18]

---

18   http://www.freetheslaves.net/about-slavery/slavery-today/
     http://www.alternet.org/civil-liberties/there-are-more-slaves-today-any-time-human-history
     http://www.wnd.com/2016/02/more-slaves-today-than-at-any-time-in-history/

Child slave labor... Yes, this practice still exists. Parents in developing countries are convinced to send their children (mostly girls) to textile mills and garment factories in exchange for the promise of food, living wages, a safe work environment, and opportunities to create a sustainable lifestyle. The reality is these children often end up as modern-day slaves working in deplorable conditions just to fulfill the need today for unskilled workers. In fact, some jobs, such as the tedious task of embroidery and beading work or picking cotton from fragile plants, are often done by children because of their small hands. Also, children are usually very easy to train and supervise, and sweatshop owners know that these children virtually have no voice. Sadly, young girls who grow up in this type environment often don't know anything else. It is perpetuated from generation to generation. A cycle of poverty is set in motion. There are literally millions of people enslaved in the fashion industry alone today.

The Parliament of the United Kingdom passed a law known as the Modern Slavery Act 2015[19] designed to tackle slavery within the U.K. (England and Wales). It is designed to ensure and address human rights issues in supply chains and consolidates previous offenses for human trafficking and slavery. This act is a step in the right direction and one all countries should take to heart and begin to implement through their own policies. Our people are our greatest natural resource and should be treated

19   http://www.legislation.gov.uk/ukpga/2015/30/contents/enacted
     https://www.theguardian.com/sustainable-business/2015/dec/14/
     modern-slavery-act-explained-business-responsibility-supply-chain
     http://www.legislation.gov.uk/ukpga/2015/30/pdfs/ukpga_20150030_
     en.pdf

with respect and dignity. The fact that anyone can STILL legally own, enslave and exploit another person for monetary gain is something that should never have been possible in the first place and should be absolutely unfathomable in society today. Are we as evolved as we think we are?

An organization by the name of Free2Work tracks and researches brands and how they do business. These brands include the ones I am sure we all frequent. They are given a grade on a scale from A to F—most are in the D range. Their goal is to keep us all informed and give us the tools and information we need to make our purchases mindfully!

"The most powerful person is the one who is awake and uses their voice against injustices in the world." — Tracey Martin

WHAT DEFINES YOUR SELF-WORTH?

"The mirror doesn't tell your whole story." — Tracey Martin

We all are prone to buying into the hype behind the latest must-haves. Who among us hasn't at one time fallen prey to the gorgeous advertisements that play into our desire to look and feel beautiful? We hope that once we put that new piece of clothing on, the reflection looking back at us will embody the attributes we see advertised: happy, skinny, wealthy, and popular. But when you really think about it, what does this message convey about us? That we are only as beautiful as the clothing we wear? This has happened to me, many of my friends, and my family members.

I LOVE fashion. I LOVE style and the way it can make me feel, and how I can make it my own. So, don't get me wrong; I am not saying we shouldn't want to look good and care about our appearance and take care of ourselves. I am simply pointing out that we have some serious work to do on the inside if we have allowed the big advertising companies and propaganda machines to fool us into measuring our self-worth by the labels we wear.

There are so many celebrity brands and large fashion houses out there who claim to want to empower the women and men who WEAR their lines. They want them to feel beautiful, sexy, and confident. But what about the people who are actually making these garments? They also have families and hopes and dreams, and their rights and needs should be considered as much as the customer's when creating a business model.

Global fashion brands are huge. With annual revenues in the billions of dollars, they are part of a $1.2 Trillion-a-year industry, with $250 Billion spent in the U.S. alone.[20] I am all for a company being successful and profitable, and when *compassionate capitalism* is put into play with integrity, everybody wins. However, the fashion industry is one of the biggest contributors to environmental decline and pollution, right along with petroleum refining and animal agriculture. It is also one of the most influential and powerful industries on the planet.

---

20 https://maloney.house.gov/sites/maloney.house.gov/files/documents/
    The%20Economic%20Impact%20of%20the%20Fashion%20
    Industry%20--%20JEC%20report%20FINAL.pdf

Three vital questions we HAVE to ask are:

1. Could this power and influence be used to shift the entire industry?

2. Are there enough honorable and integrity-based businessmen and women involved in the industry to have the fortitude to make different choices?

3. Are there enough conscious customers willing to take a stand and put their money behind ethical brands?

When it comes to fashion, it is often hard to spout statistics because factories, companies, and fashion brands aren't really keeping track of them: organic vs. conventional cotton use, water consumption rate, and chemical dye runoff—just to name a few. Building a fashion brand is a multi-layered process with many hands and "cooks in the kitchen." The brands are sophisticated when it comes to the end of the supply chain and the cutting and sewing phase because it is very tangible. All the processes that come before are not always easily tracked. This is where the industry must do better by developing better ways of tracking this information. We need better tools. In an industry that is this wealthy, it is inexcusable for the world to suffer at the hands of its lack of transparency and traceability.

WHO INFLUENCES WHAT YOU WEAR?

The onset of social media has ultimately led to an entire generation of young people who now believe they are "celebrities" in their own social media circles. They are unconsciously sending the message of more, more, more to the "fans" who look up to them as role models. But, we have to look beneath the veil to discover the real truth. My daughters have drawn my attention to young YouTubers who create "Fashion Haul" videos showcasing the excessive amount of clothing they buy in one shopping trip and implanting a gluttonous mindset into the heads of their viewers. These young adults feel this is a "normal" way to shop. Most of the garments go unworn with the tags still on them in their closet.

We see fashion bloggers in photos wearing the most amazing styles and branded couture, and we think, 'How can these 20-somethings afford these clothes?' Well, the truth is these "influencers" are either paid by a brand or given free products in the hopes that brand will receive editorial coverage or product placement in a social media post. I know this because I have done this with my own brands in the past. The only authentic way for a brand to gain celebrity coverage is when that person actually purchases the item and truly does use or wear it and loves it enough to share it with the public and their fan base.

Let's face it—we all get inspiration from others, whether it be from our best friends or maybe a fashion-forward girl crush. Either way, we look to others for ideas, and sometimes we try and find our own identity in outside influences. There is so much bombarding us on a daily basis, I am not sure if we even know what our own identity really is.

Fashion is what the powers that be dictate to us as the customers. They decide which brands are good and which are not; who makes the cut and who does not; what we should wear, when we should wear it, and even the colors we should want to wear. This honestly boggles my mind. I don't even know what

I am wearing tomorrow, let alone what I will feel like wearing next fall.

WHY DO WE BUY WHAT WE BUY?

Well, let's think along the lines of BUYOLOGY instead of Biology. What creates your shopping patterns and informs your purchases? Companies spend millions of dollars annually researching this very subject. Brands know everything about our general shopping patterns, down to whether most of us go left or right when we first enter a store. For instance, they know to place the higher priced items up front and position the sales rack in the back of the store, so you are more likely to find something you have to have in the full-priced section before you wander into the discounted area. These areas are often in disarray and not very inviting to shop through.

This same thought can be applicable while shopping online. The visuals and imagery used are meant to evoke an emotional response from the customer to encourage them to purchase. The new and most expensive items are on the first few pages while the sale items are often buried behind numerous pages of products. Sometimes the sale button is located at the end of the tool bar. You will actually have to search for it.

Ever wonder why when you walk into a retail store in the middle of summer, it's freezing inside? They aren't just pumping in the A/C to give you respite from the heat. This, like almost everything, is a strategic tactic. Because clothes are released ahead of the season, stores are filled with fall clothing in the summer. And typically, when it's a blistering 90 degrees outside, you're not going to be thinking about buying that warm winter sweater. But when you're literally shivering in your cutoff jean shorts after a few minutes in the arctic-like climate they've created, that sweater will start looking like something you need— and now! Just like that, your mindset has been altered. Kind of like shopping for a Halloween costume while grabbing a star for the top of your Christmas tree... Can we just have one season or holiday at a time, please? Can we live in the moment and honor the season we are currently in?

We are manipulated by color, as well. When we start seeing cobalt blue items in every store, even if we don't particularly care for that shade of blue, we eventually find ourselves reaching to buy everything we can in that color. Again, our mindset has been altered. The saddest part is we have lost our sense of individuality and personal style. Everyone looks the same and every store stocks the same merchandise as the next one down the street.

This movement towards stylistic conformity not only affects the individuality of the customer, but also the designer. If your clothing line doesn't fit in with the current trends, it will not be given a second look by buyers. They want what everyone else has, so their store will remain competitive. *Who is the one really following the trends at this point? Can you keep your uniqueness when you are put in a proverbial style box?*

Chapter 2

We Have to Go Deeper Than What is on the Surface...

Most large-scale brands have a business model built on a sophisticated marketing strategy that gives the appearance of a certain kind of desirable lifestyle we as customers buy into. We believe that by wearing these clothes, we will live the same lifestyle portrayed in the glossy magazine adds or flashy commercials.

However, with all the commercialization and slick advertising, we are only seeing one side of the industry. The side that sells! Most manufacturing is often done in less developed countries, so brands can drive profits through the roof while having no accountability for the mass destruction of human lives, toxic waste, and poverty they leave behind that their customers will never see.[21] We are too busy basking in the pseudo-lifestyle our new outfit has temporarily afforded us to realize its true cost.

Communication and collaboration are vital between brands and all sourcing components to create massive, scalable sustainability in the fashion industry. We need agreements between brands, manufacturers, factory owners, buyers, agents, and even local governments to properly address and enact change. All facilities need to go through regular inspections to ensure compliance with regulations put in place regarding the products and methods used to produce our clothing. And these regulations can no longer be brushed aside for the sake of profit or deadlines.

This business model for fast fashion was originally based on a double-win scenario for everyone involved. We, the customers, would get great clothing items quickly, easily and at more affordable prices, while the manufacturing countries were supposed to benefit from the economic boost in jobs, promised healthcare, and bright futures. But this business model is NOT sustainable. Unfortunately, it has been an epic failure on most levels due to human greed and misuse of power.

In order to change something, we must first admit there is a problem. It is not easy to admit that we have been part of creating it; in fact, sometimes that is the hardest part. From the brand owners to the company CEOs to the designers, and from the factory owners to the customers...

21 https://evonews.com/theforgotten/2017/jun/01/children-from-poor-countries-slaves-in-textile-factories-to-temper-the-insatiable-appetite-of-fast-fashion-consumers-from-the-west/
    https://www.environmentalleader.com/2014/10/assessing-the-environmental-impact-of-the-fashion-world/

we have all played a part. The sooner we own our individual responsibility, the sooner we can begin laying the foundation for change.

Once we have opened our eyes to the true cost of this industry, change will be inevitable. Brands will have to do better. We no longer have an option to allow these atrocities to continue to be committed against humans, animals, and the earth.

> **"We do not inherit the earth from older generations, we borrow it from our children." — Native American Proverb**

Can you live with the fact that your children or grandchildren may never see an elephant in the wild due to the extinction of these creatures in part because of the ivory trade industry? Or tigers due to the fur industry? We are doing more harm to animals than any natural predator ever would. Theirs is the circle of life. Humans were never a part of it. What about the thought that your children or grandchildren many never enjoy some of the world's natural wonders because of deterioration caused by Earth's pollution levels? Clean rivers and oceans due to the dumping of toxic waste from textile manufacturing and dyeing. We have seen this type of dystopia depicted in science fiction movies. Oftentimes, art imitates life—it just takes a while.

The fashion world is playing a huge part, on so many levels, in the climate change issue we are facing today. The industry participates in this destruction through its reliance on the use of pesticides and herbicides to grow the fibers to make fabric, as well as through the use of petrochemicals to dye and finish the fabric, both of which use fossil fuels and are a large contributor to climate change. The shipping of goods all around the world adds to the massive, growing carbon footprint the fashion industry is leaving behind. Even if you question whether climate change is real, you have to agree with the fact that clean air, clean water, and a thriving ecosystem are what we all need. This industry is negatively impacting us all.

BECOMING MINDFUL

As a designer, when I create an item, I budget everything that goes into that garment or accessory: sketching, pattern making, sampling, sourcing fabric, zippers, buttons, thread, rivets, grommets, labels, shipping and labor, etc. I think about every last detail, all the way down to the hangtags, packaging, and marketing. Each one of these components comes from somewhere and was made by someone. However, what designers and brand directors often don't think about or address is how many natural resources it takes to make one single item and its output into the environment. How much water, energy, and human toil must go into the items they design?

This doesn't even take into consideration the leather industry or the exotic animals being killed so women can carry around a specific type of handbag. There is a certain *cost of doing business* many of us are not thinking about. For example, what is the carbon footprint to produce goods in China, ship them to L.A. for finishing and packaging, send them back to distribution centers and finally, ship them to the stores so they can be placed on shelves? How can this be measured? And what should the punishment be for companies that contribute excessive amounts of toxic waste by dumping dyes, chemicals and additives into the groundwater? Toxic chemicals do not break down, and they will eventually find their way into our food sources. If there is no penalty for dumping and no incentive not to, it then becomes a question of integrity for brands, company owners, and CEOs.

I don't believe the world needs another brand doing things the same way. We need brands to be innovative with their design, fibers, sourcing, and production. We need global thought leaders who are willing to say NO more and who are choosing to do things differently—to be willing to think outside the box. Some designers are doing this, but their reach is too limited. However, they can extend their reach by collaborating and sharing information and knowledge. Collaborate, collaborate, collaborate!

Up until now, I do not think it has been a big practice for brands and fashion businesses to collaborate with one another. In today's business model, it is a must. Abundant thinking will benefit all. As brands, you can cut costs, set yourself apart, and have a bigger reach to certain markets by collaborating.

"We move ahead in life and business not by pushing, but by leading." — Tracey Martin

For as big and influential as this industry is, there are so many jaded entities that will never embrace change or help to implement it. We must be willing to be open to ideas that we may not be able to explain or understand. Drop the ego and tap back into the compassion and spirit of collaboration.

A HISTORY LESSON...

We all know blue jeans are about as American as apple pie and baseball. They have become the American uniform. In the 1970s and '80s, the jean capital of the world was El Paso, Texas. Thousands of people worked there to create jeans for brands such as Levi's, Lee, Guess, Gap, and the beloved Jordache. Eventually, other businesses started to spring up around the area. Companies did everything from manufacturing rivets, buttons, labels, and zippers to providing laundry facilities needed to finish the denim and final washings. A thriving industry was created, and it benefited the economy on every level.

Fast Fact: **The name "denim" comes from the of a sturdy fabric called "Serge de Nimes", It was initially made in Nimes, France. hence "de Nimes" - " denim". Weavers at times tried to reproduce the cotton corduroy that was famously made in the city of Genoa, in Italy, but no luck." (history of jeans - origin of the denim jean) It was Jacob Davis and Levis Strauss who invented jeans back in 1873. Levis Strauss traveled from Germany to New York back in 1851 to work with his brother in his dry goods store.**

At the same time, China and the Soviet Union had their eyes on this new freedom symbol of America, the coveted denim blue jeans. I can remember hearing stories of people traveling abroad and bringing jeans with them to sell for hundreds of dollars. (Back then, that was a lot of money!) Regis Debray, a French philosopher, once said, "There is more power in blue jeans and rock and roll than in the entire Red Army." The whole world wanted a slice of this pie! And it was on its way to them. Manufacturing facilities started popping up in China and other underdeveloped areas because of the cheap labor and fast turnaround capabilities needed to meet this rapidly expanding market.

Today, Xintang in China is the new "Denim Capital of the World." Unfortunately, blue jean manufacturing has poisoned the city's rivers with synthetic indigo dye and other toxic run-off[22] that can be seen in satellite photos from outer space. The famed Pearl River[23] in the Guangdong Province was named for all of its beautiful pearl-colored shells that lie along the bottom of the riverbed. This body of water has sustained Chinese societies for thousands of years; yet, in recent times it has become a proverbial dumping ground and wasteland due in most part to the textile and garment industries. We should all be appalled at what has become of this and other major waterways. Everything eventually flows around the world and connects us more closely than we realize. Today, one in three pairs of jeans is manufactured in China—over 300 million pairs a year.[24]

But while the country's production statistics are high, the quality of life for its people has been lowered to nearly cata-

22   https://www.theguardian.com/environment/gallery/2011/feb/09/
      pollution-china-manufacturing-towns
23   http://www.worldbank.org/en/results/2016/05/26/cleaning-up-china-
      polluted-pearl-river
24   http://www.atlasobscura.com/articles/how-the-jeans-capital-of-the-
      world-moved-from-texas-to-china

strophic levels due to the deadly cocktail of dye, bleach, detergents, and other chemical finishes released in the dye process.[25] These substances are heavy-metal based, which means they are neurotoxins, cancer-causing carcinogens, and hormone disruptors in the form of cadmium, chromium, mercury, lead, and copper. Unfortunately, they do not break down as they enter the water supply and contaminate everything they come in contact with. According to Greenpeace East Asia, 17 out of 21[26] samples of water collected from rivers in China, tested positive for these chemicals. 17 out of 21! We must do better!

Yes, I too love my blue jeans. They are part of my daily "uniform." Whether I am wearing cutoffs, bell-bottoms, skinny jeans or flares, I am in love with denim! And I know I'm not the only one who loves that beautiful blue color. I focus on being mindful though by purchasing my denim secondhand or from "Made-in-the-USA" brands. By "Made in the USA," I mean the product is fully designed and manufactured in the U.S. Were you aware a product could just be **finished** in the U.S. and still brand itself as "Made in the USA"? We need better definitions!

The indigo dyes used on denim can come from synthetic sources, as well as natural ones. Natural indigo is an organic compound with a beautiful, distinct blue color. There is historical proof that shows natural indigo dates all the way back to 1600–2400 B.C. in Egyptian artifacts. It is also found in items

---

25   https://www.theguardian.com/global-development-professionals-network/2017/jun/02/china-water-dangerous-pollution-greenpeace
     http://www.scmp.com/news/china/policies-politics/article/1935314/80-cent-groundwater-chinas-major-river-basins-unsafe
26   http://www.greenpeace.org/eastasia/news/stories/toxics/2010/textile-pollution-xintang-gurao/

from India, Indonesia, and China around that same time. The natural dyes are extracted from a few different species of indigo plants through an arduous process, but primarily, from the Indigofera plant. Typically, the cotton threads are soaked and dried 15–20 times in indigo dye to achieve the level of color of our favorite jeans. So take care of the ones you own!

Sometimes labels are a good thing.

> **"Symptoms of a broken industry or broken body will remain in place to teach us a lesson. Accept the lessons and create a prescription for change."** — Tracey Martin

Here is a fun exercise: Imagine if every time you purchased clothing, you were informed of what your clothes were made of, where they were made and who made them. In the spirit of full transparency, I decided to create a clothing nutrition label showing the ingredients—the "calories," "proteins," "fats," and "carbs"— contained in a pair of jeans. What might this clothing nutrition label

Nutrition Facts	
Serving Size: 1 Pair of Jeans	
Serving Per Package: 1	
Amount Per Serving	**Denim Jeans**
Calories	**$275.00**
Carlories from Fat	Skinneys
Formaldehyde	42%
Lead	3%
Water	1800 gallons
Human Labor	
Sodium Hydroxide	
Carcinogen	10%
Child Labor	12 years old
By Products of Indigo Synthesis	
Ammonia	
Sulfuric Acid	
Sodium Hydroxide	
Non-renewable Resources	
Coal Energy	
Origin:	**China**

look like on your favorite pair? Keep in mind this is a mock label to prove a point!

Seeing this kind of information on a label would make you think twice about purchasing this product, right? Remember, every dollar spent is a vote for a brand to either continue doing bad business as usual or change its practices to adopt a more ethical and sustainable business model. When we educate ourselves and our families, we truly become empowered so that we have the confidence to ask the right questions and make the ethical purchases that will benefit all parties.

"I would rather ask powerful questions and risk offending someone than not ask and have regrets." — Tracey Martin

---

Chapter 3

From Dirt to Shirt
and Back Again

SUSTAINABILITY IS OUR COLLECTIVE RESPONSIBILITY

Have you ever heard the saying, "Give a man a fish, and you feed him for a day; show him how to catch fish, and you feed him for a lifetime?" Teaching someone a skill or craft instills them with knowledge, dignity, and self-confidence. Knowing they can sustain a certain way of life for themselves, their family, and their community is an invaluable feeling.

Sustainability (for our purposes in this book) is defined as the conservation of all living things through the ecological balance of humankind, animals, oceans, plants, and our ecosystem. Therefore, anything that comes from the ground should also return to the ground. Foreign or manmade substances do more harm to our ecosystem than we can ever imagine, and that damage is becoming more and more visible at a disturbing rate. We can only push Mother Nature so far until she starts to push back. She gives us everything—water for drinking, plants for eating and medicinal use, air for breathing, and breathtaking scenery to help us enjoy our time on Earth. We still haven't gotten the message that this is our home, and it's the only one we will have. We need to learn to live in harmony with every living thing that resides here with us. And remember, not from a place of control and dominance, but from a place of stewardship.

Fast Fact: **Plastic was invented in 1907. It takes 450 years for plastic to biodegrade, and some plastic bottles may take up to 1,000 years.**[27] **This means that EVERY piece of plastic ever made is still on this planet!**

Plastic can be used for so much. There are wonderful companies collecting plastic from the ocean floors and repurposing it for fashion and accessories. This is a great idea, since it seems that it will be around for a verrrryyyy loooooong time. We actually should not have to produce any more plastic IF we recycle what is already here. What a great opportunity for creative and innovative minds to really start to harness this abundant resource!

Public Service Announcement: The truth is plastic is in every one of us, as well as most animals and fish on the planet. We all have petrochemical waste in our bodies. The plastic gets thrown away and makes its way to the oceans and our waterways. Fish then eat the plastic, and we eat the fish. What we

27   http://www.postconsumers.com/education/how-long-does-it-take-a-plastic-bottle-to-biodegrade/

use for about 15 minutes and then throw away is never really "thrown away." What does that really mean? Where is "away"? Plastic lasts for hundreds of years. But, I will save all of this for another book. This issue is a rabbit hole and a half once you enter it! Don't even get me started on the Great Pacific Garbage Patch[28]...! Mini-rant over; back to matters at hand.

A self-sustaining system is one that does not take more from the environment than it is giving back. This type of system does not deplete resources, but rather, is able to sustain itself. For example, a natural lake is a sustainable system. It does not need any outside influence to continue to survive and regenerate. It is able to produce everything it needs within its own ecosystem. Even after they have been polluted, some rivers are able to regenerate their ecosystems over time.

> *"Mother Nature will heal herself. She just needs an invitation to do so." — Tracey Martin*

So, you are probably asking yourself, "What does this have to do with the fashion industry and the clothes in my closet?" It means that the design, sourcing, manufacturing, and production of garments should not pollute the environment or deplete and destroy our natural resources. When the life of the garment comes to an end, it should be absorbed back into the environment as best as possible and cause no harm. Think of the phrase, "From dirt to shirt and back again."

---

28 https://www.nationalgeographic.org/encyclopedia/great-pacific-garbage-patch/

For true change and sustainability to become commonplace in the fashion world (and in our daily lives), customers must be educated, emotionally moved, and have a sense of social and ethical responsibility. I, for one, am not willing to leave it up to the big brands and the powers that be. It is clear they are having trouble making basic decisions for the good of humanity. In order to realize a large-scale change across this vast and very powerful commercial industry, we as customers must care enough and DEMAND it!

We all say we want change. We say we want people to be treated fairly and have their basic needs met. We say we love our planet and all the creatures that inhabit it. But are you willing to be one of the millions of people we need to follow through on those words? Can you sustain the integrity of your word and values, while you are standing in front of a clothing rack and getting ready to purchase this year's "IT" item? You may have the best of intentions when you leave your house to go shopping, but can you make the right decision at the register? There is actually a name for this phenomenon—it's called the Intention-Behavior Gap. Yay! Yet another label for our inability to be held accountable for our actions!

> *"We are spending millions of dollars to see if there is life on other planets, while we are spending billions of dollars destroying this one." — Prince Ea*

After reading about all the challenges currently plaguing the fashion industry, you might be asking yourself, "But what can *I* do?" While the problem may seem overwhelmingly bigger than ourselves, we can't become paralyzed thinking there's nothing we can do. Sometimes when we see things that move us emotionally, we feel helpless, but we never truly are in these situations. The truth is we are just beginning to wake up to reality and learn more about why and how we got here. There can be no pointing fingers because we all have participated in the demise of our species and the planet on some level. The good news is those of us who are finally aware can collaborate and band together to create true, lasting change while helping to awaken the rest of society. We CAN do this together!

> *"Once we know the truth, we must become mobilized into action instead of paralyzed by complacency." — Tracey Martin*

SMALL CHANGES CAN CREATE HUGE MOVEMENTS IN THE RIGHT DIRECTION.

However, this kind of change will not magically happen overnight. Consumerism is embedded into our culture. If you wake up on Monday and say you will NEVER buy fast fashion again, or you won't get sucked into buying more items than you need, you are probably not being realistic. The idea is to create changes in your purchasing habits that you can sustain over a lifetime and to teach your family and friends to do the same.

These cultural changes have been happening throughout humanity's existence. The shift must happen in the minds of each one of us as to how we define "the good life." Where does your joy come from? Where does your sense of success come from?

"To create a liberating and free life means to let go of material things and pursue fulfilling relationships, calm and a centered sense of self."— Tracey Martin

We must learn how to become more conscious shoppers; how to become more sophisticated when it comes to knowing the brands we are supporting, who makes our clothes, how they are made, what they are made of, and what the impact is. Being mindful of our own ecological footprint on the planet and realizing that everything we do has an effect on someone or something else is vital to our survival. We are all in this together!

"We must awaken to the fact that what we do to others, we do to ourselves." — Tracey Martin

I believe consumer habits are one of the most important cogs in the wheel of change. Brands will get the message loud and clear if we commit to sending the right one. Today, quite a few companies have information on their websites that pertain to "sustainability," but it can often be hard to find.

HERE ARE SOME GREAT EXAMPLES OF SUSTAIN-ABILITY IN ACTION:

Let's use H&M as the first example. Unfortunately, when you go to their site, it is not readily visible. You actually have to type in www.sustainability.hm.com.[29] What if the "sustainability" button was right next to the "shop" button? The website states, "We are committed to transparent reporting on our sustainability performance." It goes on to state, "Sustainability starts at the drawing board. We need to create fashion without compromising on design, quality, price, and sustainability." This company is a massive ship that seems to be trying to move in the right direction. However, it is never fast enough for those of us that are working to see change. The bigger the company, the bigger the resources and the bigger their leaps toward sustainability should be. The truth is, we are probably five years away from even having an industry-wide standard of what "sustainability" really means and the tools to measure it accurately.

So, the answer for some of the bigger brands who are addressing "sustainability" now is what they are calling "takeback" or recycling programs. In the case of H&M, they have implemented a recycling program for their clothing. You can drop off your unwanted garments, no matter the brand, to the closest store near you. They say they are committed to giving them a new life or sending them on to be recycled. They have also put social projects in place and are teaming up with organizations such as The Hong Kong Research Institute of Textiles and Ap-

---

29 http://sustainability.hm.com/en/sustainability/about/about/ceo-message.html

parel to develop new technologies for these recycled clothes to be made into new garments and accessories.[30]

Eileen Fisher brand has put their own twist on this concept. They have developed a program called Fisher Found (previously known as Green Eileen) that gives your clothing another life after you've enjoyed it. You can bring items back to Eileen Fisher stores, and they will find them a new home or redesign them completely. To make it more enticing for you, they will give you a $5 reward card. If you have trouble finding a location, visit them online for more instructions: www.eileenfisher.com

THE PLANET SHOULDN'T HAVE TO PAY FOR YOUR BIG DAY.

Some of the most beautiful rituals that we have participated in for thousands of years can be the most taxing on our environment. They can be the most mindless form of consumption that we participate in.

Your wedding day... so special and so beautiful. Have you ever thought about the fact this one day that takes so much preparation, thought, detail, and fabric is also so incredibly wasteful? I love the idea of a big wedding. However, it seems like such a waste in today's world. We put so much thought and planning into the "day," but not so much thinking about the planet, relationship, and our future.

---

30 http://www.hkrita.com/en-us/about-us/about-hkrita
    Textile Waste Recycling by Biological Method: http://www.itf.gov.hk/l-eng/prj_Profile2.asp?code=DB9F3261C4E16DECF00CB5E0D74DA5F33 519414AA51550D0C243BC277EC17481

Sustainability is a great topic to include in the conversation before planning your wedding. The average cost of a wedding dress today is $1,564.[31] However, a typical dress can range from $1,500 to $10,000 and beyond! This doesn't even take into account dresses for bridesmaids, mothers of the bride and groom, flower girls, and whatever your guests purchase to wear. Now, factor in table linens, napkins, and silk flowers. Whew! That's a lot of fabric and cost. The groom and groomsmen have it right by renting their tuxes!

I have even seen brides purchase a couple of different gowns for their wedding day. They possibly wear each one for a few hours and then what...? Maybe get them organically (hopefully) dry cleaned and put in a frame? Or, more likely, put them in a bag stored in a spare bedroom closet.

Below are a few words from Jeanne Hankerson of SJ Couture, a wonderful bridal designer, speaking on sustainability in the wedding gown world,

"Sustainability is a core value written into our mission statement and vision. From its inception as a brand, SJ has and continues to be designed and produced in the USA. Inspired by vintage style, each piece is meant to be re-worn, re-used, and passed down. We will recreate your wedding dress after your big day so it can live in your daily wardrobe. SJ must keep sustainability in mind at all times—because each dress is crafted to endure. We choose to use natural fibers—silk and cotton—and eco-friendly materials such as hemp and lace from recycled plastic. No synthetics or toxic chemical dyes means not only

---

31   https://www.theknot.com/content/average-cost-of-wedding-dress-2016

will the gowns last for generations, but that they are also in harmony with the environment and nature."

For more info visit www.sjcouture.com

Each one of these examples is displaying the business owner's personal belief and values on sustainability. What would it look like if every company implemented forward thinking when it came to their sustainability practices within their own company culture and industry?

Chapter 4

Nurturing the Global Marketplace

"If you can reach people, you can inspire change." — Tracey Martin

Somewhere along the path of global human evolution, we seem to have veered off course. We've become numb to tragic images and stories we see on the news every day and immune to the constant stream of social media messages blowing up our cellphones day and night. Our news feeds are filled with negative narrative—strangers arguing about politics, race and economic development and further fueling hatred and intolerance. And what is the result? We shut down. We internalize our world outlook, and consequently, we become so concerned with what WE want that we don't care HOW we get it. Here in the Western world, our massive consumerism attitude is wreaking havoc on animals, earth, and other human beings all over the world. However, we don't see it, so we do not believe it is happening. And we definitely can't see how we have participated. We have such a huge problem with things being manufactured in China; however, aren't our closets full of products from there?

What if you were forced to switch places with a garment factory worker for a week? Would you stand for the injustices of low wages, unsafe working conditions, and compromised health? I think not! Some people may reason, "But what would happen if we stop buying? At least, we are giving them jobs." That logic is inherently false. Supplying someone with a job that cannot be sustained is not creating an economic lifeline to lift them out of poverty. There are better ways to help.

For instance, if we were all willing to pay only $1–2 more for a shirt, it would equate to an increase in worker welfare. To this, people may retort, "But what if the factory owner doesn't pass the extra revenue along to their employees?" Great question, and one that should be thrown back to buying agents of the brands. They need to ensure the extra revenue makes it to the workers through the contracts they put in place with the man-ufacturing companies. Stiff fines must be implemented and reinforced when any fundamental business practice is not fol-lowed. A change of heart must begin within the decision mak-ers at every level of the industry. I don't think any of us asked these brands to produce cheap clothing. I don't think we said, "Can you please make me a pair of jeans that will fall apart after four washings, and while you are at it, only pay your workers pennies for their labor?" Wrong!

So then, how can we as customers create a better global marketplace? How can we transform into a compassionate capitalist market? Is this even possible? I say, YES it is! One thing we can do is bring some of the manufacturing back to the U.S. Not only will this help our economy, but it will also lessen the carbon footprint on exports and bring some awareness to "how" we do business. It will also force factories to take a long, hard look at their current manufacturing practices. Most customers walk into a store with no idea how the products they are about to purchase got there.[32] So, while it is up to the brands to develop more of a collective conscience, it is also up to us, the customer, to become responsible influencers in the global marketplace as well.

We simply need to look beyond the clothing racks at the local mall to find beautiful garments with true character and history. Indigenous people from around the world create some of the most beautiful textiles, beading, and craftsmanship that you will never find in a department store. Their cultures have fostered and nurtured the art of crafting for thousands of years. They didn't ask for us to pollute their environment or take over their land. They just want to live their lives and feed their families. Is there a way to work WITH other cultures to honor, and

---

32 http://www.scmp.com/magazines/post-magazine/article/1970431/true-cost-your-cheap-clothes-slave-wages-bangladesh-factory
http://money.cnn.com/2015/05/22/news/economy/true-cost-clothing/index.html

at the same time, celebrate their heritage? I believe the answer is a resounding YES!

When we purchase from sustainable and ethical brands, these are often the people those brands work with. Brand founders travel the world to study how they might be able to positively impact a village or city by providing a chance for its inhabitants to sell their goods through an online marketplace, or by setting up a micro-lending or financing chain, so the workers are ensured fair wages. Most of us want to support other cultures and to be able to purchase something that comes from a faraway land. Support what they do without changing it. Honor their art and pay fair wages for it. These people have passed on their craft from generation to generation. However, this way of life is in danger of becoming extinct. Younger generations do not want to continue it because they believe it is not profitable, and they are probably correct. They see how the older generations are selling their art for a minuscule amount of money just to feed their families, and they don't want to go down the same path to poverty. We can help with this when we pay fair trade wages for items we purchase.

IT *IS* A SMALL WORLD AFTER ALL

When we look at some of the most beautiful textiles in the world, we are also getting a geography lesson. In many parts of the world, textiles are a vital element of the culture. People tell stories while using rare fibers and generations old artisan methods to create clothing and goods. This to me is luxury: knowing that someone has created a product with their hands and it has positively impacted their economy, while not harming the environment. Beautiful woven textiles come from places like Guatemala, Bali, Ghana, Chile, Turkey, and Peru, just to name a few. As customers, we must educate ourselves on buying authentic products and avoiding knockoffs made in un-ethical shops halfway around the world. Cultural diversity is a beautiful thing to celebrate, and one way we can do this is by purchasing textiles and wares on trips abroad and decorating our homes with them. Oh, the stories they will tell!

GUATEMALA

One of the most gorgeous weaving traditions in the world is rooted here, and the fabric options are very diverse. These fabrics represent a rich history rooted in Mayan culture and honoring Mother Nature and the conservation of water and life forms. The indigenous people here have an exceptional talent for weaving, and they use many different colors and styles of fabric. Women in the villages make beautiful pieces for family members or to give as gifts. Each piece is special and made with a lot of sweat and love and generational influence.

BALI

Bali is known for traditional Batik finishes that are achieved when wax-resistant dye is applied to a whole cloth, an ancient art form that has been around for thousands of years. Wax covers the fabric you don't want to be colored, and the rest of the uncovered fabric absorbs the dye, resulting in a beautiful, unique look. Batiking is a major part of Balinese history. Be sure to purchase original Batik though, not a knockoff made in an unethical facility. Learn to read labels and determine the place of origin before buying.

GHANA

This West African country is rich in textile history dating back to 5,000 B.C. and features woven cotton in rich, vibrant colors derived from natural plants, flowers, and fruits. Often, patterns created on kente cloth, the national fabric, will depict beautiful geometrical patterns, figures, and shapes. The continent of Africa is also rich in alternative fibers—some come from the bark of trees, like Ugandan bark cloth taken from the Mutuba tree. The bark is stripped from the tree, and the tree is then wrapped with its own leaves so the bark can regenerate. The bark is then stretched and beaten until it becomes a "hide" of sorts, similar to leather. It can be used to make handbags, wallets, shoes, and even the interior of cars. This is a time-honored tradition that must continue for the indigenous people there.

CHILE

This South American country's textile industry[33] has grown by leaps and bounds, but its history is rich in cultural tradition. The first fabrics here were made from animal skin and hair. Since then, they have evolved to using cotton, wool, and vibrantly dyed yarns woven on huge looms to create scarves, blankets, and ponchos that will last for generations to come!

---

33 http://www.fibre2fashion.com/industry-article/7418/investors-paradise-chile-apparel-textile

TURKEY

This country has a virtual plethora of fabric history![34] Turkish rugs, bedding, towels, and robes are some of the world's most coveted luxury items. Collecting pieces like these and bringing them home to remind you of your travels beats a cheap t-shirt from a tourist trap (probably made in China anyway!).

PERU

Like the countries mentioned above, Peru is also rich in textile heritage. This country boasts some of the most stylish products woven from alpaca wool. These beautiful hats, gloves, scarves, ponchos, blankets, and other home goods are woven and dyed using traditional methods by villagers high in the Andes Mountains. Purchasing some of these pieces means you are empowering artisans and contributing to this nation's economy. What you get is a piece of a culture rich in tradition and Peruvian identity.

If you are fortunate enough to be able to experience traveling to these faraway places, maybe veer off the beaten path from typical tourist groups and shop where the locals shop to find the best goods these countries have to offer. If the only travel you are able to do is through the internet and your computer, no problem. You can find many of these items through online outlets.

---

34   https://www.fashionatingworld.com/new1-2/turkish-textile-industry-looking-to-rebound-in-2017

NURTURING NATURE

Unfortunately, not all fabrics have been protected so that they retain their full integrity. Take, for instance, one of the most beautiful and luxurious fibers on the planet, *cashmere*. The best quality cashmere comes from Mongolia, and boy did it use to be spectacular! The goats there are typically humanely tended to by nomadic herders and grow soft, think coats due to living in high altitudes and extremely frigid temperatures in winter. Historically, they roamed the land freely and were then brought in for shearing in early Spring. The shearing was done with the utmost precision and care to ensure no harm came to the animals. The villagers who did the shearing took pride and care in these animals because they valued what was being taken from them and knew these animals were a huge source of financial stability and economic growth for their community. Each goat typically produced enough fleece to make 4 oz. of cashmere. To put that in perspective, an average sheep might provide enough fleece for 3–4 sweaters. So, you can see why cashmere was considered a luxury fiber.

Fast forward to today. You can purchase cashmere at Walmart for about $54.99 per sweater. Its quality is declining at the same rate as the humane treatment of these majestic animals. They are often treated as poorly as the other animals who have become victims of the factory farming industry. China is now one of the largest suppliers of cashmere. Unfortunately, they are blending other fibers and hairs in with the cashmere, like camel hair, due to the overwhelming demand and lack of supply. The cashmere pills, wears holes and doesn't have the same luxurious feel it used to. We have consumed it at such a rapacious rate that we have ruined this beautiful fiber as well. Rules and regulations put in place are completely ignored, so the factories can meet the demands of the brands and ultimately the appetite of the "I want it all NOW!" customer.

Seeing how this exploitation can happen in almost any industry, however, tells me that we have much more than a supply and demand problem. This is a humanity problem. It is a systemic failure of a once thriving system caused by the moral decline of the people behind the brands. The art of true fashion must be brought back. The brands that are doing things ethically, sustainably, and through Fair Trade should be rewarded with your dollars so they can continue to influence the industry and create change by implementing a business model that takes all costs into consideration and limits waste. The fashion industry knows this and is striving to change. I commend the industry for being willing to open up and look for alternatives and better ways to do business. However, the process needs to be expedited and action needs to be implemented now!

LOST IN FIBERS (NATURAL, OF COURSE)

Some fibers used in fabric are better than others. There are certain ones I encourage you to look for. Conventionally grown cotton, as we learned in the previous chapters, is not something that we necessarily want next to our skin. It uses more pesticides than any other crop in the world. Cotton makes up a third of fiber consumption in the textile industry according to a global consumption report published in 2016.[35] Also, the Scientific American reported that in the US, more than 10,000 people die each year from cancer-related chemical exposure.[36] To make things worse for our ecosystem, the U.S. Fish and Wildlife Service has found that pesticides kill at least 67 million birds annually![37] The chemicals from the farms run off and enter our lakes, rivers, and waterways. Pesticide residue is found in food, farm animals, and even human breast milk! These carcinogens cause cancer in adults but have an extremely harmful effect on growing young children. These children can develop crippling neurological conditions.

Please look for these fibers when reading the labels on your clothing and when you are shopping for yourself and your family.

Organic Cotton – This beautiful fiber[38] has not been genetically modified. No herbicides and pesticides or synthetic chemicals have been used in the growing of the plant. Organic cotton can come from the USA, Turkey, China, and India. It uses far less water than conventional cotton and is far less harmful for our health and the health of our planet.

---

35 http://www.lenzing.com/en/investors/equity-story/global-fiber-market.html

36 https://www.scientificamerican.com/article/how-many-cancers-are-caused-by-the-environment/

37 http://www.defenders.org/sites/default/files/publications/pesticides_and_endangered_wildlife.pdf

https://www.theorendatribe.com/blogs/the-orenda-tribe/organic-cotton-recycled-material-eco-friendly-fashion-does-it-really-matter

38 https://www.organicfacts.net/organic-cotton-clothing.html

https://www.organiccotton.org/oc/Organic-cotton/Benefits-of-organic-cotton/Benefits-of-oc.php

Baby Alpaca – Is soft, durable, luxurious, and has a silky hand feel. It is much warmer than sheep wool and has no lanolin. Perfectly hypoallergenic means that it is suitable for the most sensitive skin. This fiber is also naturally water repellent. The hand feel of this gorgeous fiber rivals the most expensive cashmere.

Hemp – (the kind you wear) – The fiber comes from the long strands of the hemp plant, otherwise known as the bast fibers. These are the best fibers for manufacturing textiles because they can be spun into a woven linen like fabric at a very fine gauge. The plant itself has a multitude of uses within a sustainable way of life. It can be used in cleaning products, paper, cosmetics, bedding, furniture, and shoes. Also, hemp is one of the strongest fibers used to produce rope.

Linen – This beautiful yarn is derived from the stalks of the flax plant and is one of the oldest cultivated plants in human history! The only down side is that it is an annual plant, so it only has one growing season a year. The plant consumes less water to grow which is always a plus in today's world of mindful water consumption.

Silk – This natural fiber is mostly composed of fibroin and comes from the larvae that form in the cocoon. These worms do not have to be killed to harvest the silk, although some commercially produced silk producers do steam the cocoon to kill the pupae inside. Look for peace silk instead.

Tencel – The proper name of this fiber is called Lyocell. However, you probably recognize the term **tencel** as this is the brand name for the fiber. It has a hand feel that reminds you of butter! This fiber is made from the cellulose extracted from the awesome plant, **Eucalyptus**. The fiber helps to regulate your temperature and is hypoallergenic. The bonus is that it is good for the environment and consumes less water for growth. These trees are cut rather than uprooted so they can grow back faster. The wood pulp is dissolved in a non-toxic chemical and reduced to a cellulose viscous solution. The solution is then extruded through the fine holes to create the fiber and spun into fabric. Almost 99% of the chemical, water, and waste is reused in a unique closed loop system. Now you know why we love it!

SOME NEW KIDS ON THE BLOCK

Keep your eyes out for these unique and impactful fibers. There are a few brands in the shopping section that have products created from them.

MuSkin – A Vegan "leather" that is made entirely from the mushroom plant. WHAT? It is 100% biodegradable vegetal leather that is extracted from the cap of the mushrooms. This unique fiber is tanned through a chemical free process. The hand feel is much like suede. So we will be patiently waiting for this to be ready. Unfortunately, we haven't been able to get our hands on this one yet. But we are still working on it! Shroom skin! Fabulous!

Pinatex – This one is extremely exciting! It is a hearty fiber that mimics leather and is spun from the waste of the pineapple fibers. It was discovered in the Philippines and was used in an array of textiles. More recently, it is used in everything from shoes to backpacks, and from watch bands to everyday handbags.

Banana Silk – Yes, you read this correctly. Silk made from the waste of bananas. The stalk of a banana plant contains fibrous strands that can be processed into a silk fabric or even paper. This fiber has been used in Japanese culture since the 13th century. Because it is used from the waste product of the food industry, it is a complete sustainable fiber and another circular economy product.

Nettle Fiber - Wild himalayan nettle is the purest fiber available on the market due to its remote growing range and absence of chemicals in all layers of creation. Nettle fiber is both antimicrobial and hypoallergenic as well as being highly regarded as medicinal in both Eastern and Western cultures. Additionally, as a fiber crop it sequesters carbon from the environment placing it into long term soil storage making it a truly eco friendly fiber. Nettle is known as natures multivitamin. It is rich in a variety of essential vitamins, mineral, amino acids and phytochemicals.

WE DO HAVE OPTIONS...

Putting money into research for these kinds of fibers is like putting money into cancer research for the prevention of cancer. Do not wait until you are sick and then try to cure it. The health of our world is already compromised due to the toxicity of the fashion industry. Let's start shifting now while we have time.

Human and animal lives, as well as the environment, must be respected. I pray that each person is moved to do their part. Whether you are moved by emotion or education, it really doesn't matter. Remember, even the smallest change can have a monumental effect when enacted by millions of people. Think of an orchestra. Every instrument is needed to complete the piece of music. WE are all instruments in the orchestra of humanity. Play your part!

"99 is not 100, and that single one makes a difference" – Wasteland documentary

Chapter 5

Redefining Luxury, Today and in the Future

ARE WE "FASHIONABLY IMPOVERISHED"?

"Treasures from around the world, created with craftsmanship and unique materials, are true luxuries to me." — Tracey Martin

Today, many fashion influencers are obsessed with the idea of what they believe to be "luxury." They wear only the chicest labels—Louis Vuitton, Prada, Gucci, Balenciaga, and Dior—maybe because they love the designs or maybe so they can feel like they are a part of an elite group. When did luxury become equated only with a high price tag, glossy magazines, and beautiful people? What about the faces of the workers behind the brands or the quality of the clothing, bags, and shoes? When did wearing a certain label become a way for us to feel worthy, valued or confident?

Fast Fact: **Almost 40% of the Japanese population owns at least one designer clothing item or accessory. Louis Vuitton is the most popular brand.**

Think about this for a minute...

A gentleman halfway around the world leaves his humble home and walks to his workplace in a small, cramped shop. He takes pride in his work, a craft that has been taught and passed down from generation to generation. A few thousand miles away in another developing country, a young mother leaves her children behind to go to a hut and begins the arduous task of weaving fabric by hand. Both individuals complete their work with so much attention to detail; the word disposable doesn't even exist in their world. Everything has value, and they leave a little bit of themselves and their personal story in every item they craft.

WE HAVE ALL BEEN DUPED!

A 20-something girl saves her money so she can buy a beautiful status symbol bag made (notice I said a "status symbol" not "luxury") by Louis Vuitton, Chanel, Versace or some other luxury label. Now, she believes she has made it. Now, she is in the "IN" crowd. Everyone will like her, and she feels oh, so confident! Did anything really change about HER? *(Other than her wallet is about $2,000 –$3000 lighter?)* She is still the same person inside and outside. She has the same job, same personality, and same outlook on life. So why is it we think hanging a certain designer handbag from our arm will afford us a luxurious lifestyle? Most of these purchases are not made with the idea of "investing" in quality, durability or longevity. They are made from an "ideal" the purchaser perceives an item will bring to their life. Perception is an interesting concept. You have a designer bag but can't pay your electric bill? Hmmm... What's wrong with this picture?

<u>Fast Fact:</u> **Some "lower-end" handbags are produced in the same factories as luxury handbags by the same exact workers in the same exact sweatshop conditions. When I was producing my handbag line, my agent sourced a manufacturing facility in China that made Coach bags. The bags that he saw being made, cost about $67 USD each and the retail price the brand charged was around $595. You pay for the label, not the craftsmanship of the item!**

BACK IN THE DAY...

I love the idea of what Louis Vuitton created back in 1854 in Paris. He started by designing and producing a beautiful travel trunk with every detail painstakingly taken into consideration. Each rivet, stitch, and buckle was put in place by hand and made to withstand the test of time. The brand and its offerings expanded from there. These trunks were created with craftsmanship, only the best materials were used, and they were usually made for the wealthier or more discerning clientele. They were rare and hard to find. Many of today's luxury brands were founded centuries ago by one artisanal visionary soul who began creating products by hand that were manu-factured mindfully and slowly. These brands are a part of the fashion industry's DNA, its lifeline and part of the history that this industry, we love so much, was built on. What would Louis say if he knew the state of the industry today?

"Sustainability IS Luxury" — Chere Di Boscio, Editor in Chief, Eluxe magazine

For centuries, the luxury part of the fashion industry was comprised of small family-owned companies that produced beautiful products made with the finest materials. It was con-sidered a "niche" business.

I don't know what went wrong. Well, actually, I do. It has been called the "democratization" of the luxury market. The brands lost their way when they got greedy and decided to market to the masses. Marketing executives would play up the story of the company's authentic heritage or otherwise known as their brand story and claim that they were still manufacturing this same way.

This statement evokes images like we see within the dairy industry propaganda. You know, the beautiful happy cows, la-zily grazing in a beautiful lush green pasture. They are lovingly milked by hand or a gentle machine. NO WAY!

Some of the most coveted luxury products are now made in assembly line style factories in China, Vietnam, and Korea, despite the constant insisting that they are made the "original way." You may have to dig very deep through the bag to find the tag "Made in China." You will usually find it hiding at the bottom of an inside pocket or stamped somewhere on the back side of a flap or strap. It is required of all brands to note the place of origin. However, some brands think they are exempt from this regulation. In fact, 90 percent of the bag can be made in China or another country, and only the last details such as a handle or closures being attached is done in the craftsman studio in Italy and they will attach a "Made in Italy" tag to the bag. These brands are no longer selling the dream of luxury. They are just pushing low-cost items of the namesake brands at a high profit and are wrapping them in sexy logos to entice the masses. (I spent hours on end in the local department stores looking for the *place of origin* labels on high-end labels and they were VERY difficult to find. Try it for yourself!)

> ***"Sustainable craftsmanship will endure when companies are run with integrity."***
> ***— Tracey Martin***

Luxury brands are capable of making their products at a high quality of craftsmanship and at reasonable prices. They just don't have to as long as we continue to shop blindly.

Merriam-Webster defines luxury as:

1. **A condition or situation of great comfort, ease, and wealth**
2. **Something that is expensive and NOT necessary**
3. **Something that is helpful or welcome and is not usually or always available**

This last definition: SOMETHING THAT IS HELPFUL OR WELCOME AND IS NOT USUALLY OR ALWAYS AVAILABLE... Isn't this what luxury should be when it comes to tangible items? Of course, to put things in perspective, even water can be a luxury to people in other parts of the world. A luxury item is something that is hard to find, rare and special; something we should take care of and value. If that is the case, what is special about handbags and clothes that are on every person, on every street corner, made through slave labor with cheap materials? An item loses its uniqueness when this happens.

Think about your favorite song. When you first hear it, you can't get enough...then the radio station plays it over and over and over again until you can't stand the sound of it. Then it's like nails on a chalkboard! So why is fashion any different? What is the age when we start to shift our perspective and begin to value what we buy? To seek out unique items and create our own style. Is it an age or a state of mind? Is this a value we are taught or something we acquire over time? At what age do we not want to be like "everyone else" and at what age do we want to define our own authentic style?

Task — Here is a great exercise you can do on your own. Define Style vs. Fashion and Price vs. value in your own way.

PRETTY WOMAN MOMENT

The shopping experience in luxury brand flagship stores is something like dealing with the secret service. Standing at the front door will usually be a man in a dark suit with ear devices in both ears, and his facial expression is less than inviting; it's actually very intimidating. Once you decide to enter the store, the beautiful lighting and sexy display cases speak to you and you are sucked into the experience of being treated the way you believe a "wealthy and privileged" person must be treated, right? It can be intoxicating. You feel like the salesperson values you, and not just the money you are about to plunk down.

Then you see it—the holy grail of handbags! It is in the center of the store in its own glass case with a halo of lighting illuminating its very essence. Is this the rare Hope Diamond sitting in the Smithsonian Institute? No, it is the latest season's "it" bag that just seduced you to the point you will be bringing it home, even if you must put it on three different credit cards. Don't even ask, because these bags NEVER go on sale! If you have to ask, you can't afford it is the message. That's cute that you were looking for a coupon! Now, you have your badge of luxury you can carry throughout the rest of the mall to show people you have arrived, or at least that you are part of the "in crowd." But what does this mean? For each person, it means something different. Only you can decide what it means to you.

What you buy, wear, and carry reflects what you want people to think about you. Our economic and social standing in society can be reflected through our outward appearance, but is it authentic or is it just something we want to project because we think it makes people like us? Are you "faking it" just to fit in?

Can luxury be defined by a certain product or experience? Does it define success when we can go to the mall and "spoil" or "reward" ourselves. Have we lost sight of the true definition of what luxury is? And the true value of what we buy? Millennials today are moving away from purchasing "things" and instead are looking at immersive experiences that will give the feeling of luxury. Whether it be attending a polo match where the horses might be outfitted in Hermes tack or sailing a yacht around the latest "hidden" vacation spot.

History, legacy, and tradition are words that describe luxury. Craftsmanship, artisan-made, and slow-crafted define the manufacturing practices. In essence, we are actually saving money, and it is a more sustainable purchase when we decide to buy better and buy less. Buy fewer and finer things! We will have an item longer and value it more, which means we will take care of it.

I think about my mom telling me she used to have one beautiful winter coat and it might last 10 years. It was expensive if you look at it short-term. But, over time, it was a more affordable option and better for the workers and environment as well. Think about years ago, a washer and dryer would last 20 years. Now they are built to break down in seven years, then dumped in landfills. There are things we use (handbags, shoes, clothes, etc.) and there are things we use up (toothpaste, makeup, food, etc.). Likewise, we should use fashion, not use it up.

What if we became *more* materialistic? Before you protest, let's reframe this word to mean we take better care of our material things. We actually value them and protect the ones we have, not keep disposing of them only to purchase more and more. They will last longer and serve their purpose. We must lose this disposable mindset when it comes to our clothes.

ARROGANCE OR DISCERNMENT? REFRAMING OUR EGO.

Ever since I was in my teens, I have eaten organic, healthy, whole foods; worked out at least four days a week; and was an advocate for wellness. I studied so many books, took courses, and expanded my knowledge in this area on every level. I discovered at a young age that my health and wellness truly is my only wealth in this world.

When I would bring my own food to parties or meetings, people would always say, "What's wrong with our food? Do you think you are too good to eat this food?" But I always thought this kind of attitude said more about the other person than it did about me. I was making choices FOR my health, not against them.

The same can be said about fashion. Along with our mindsets, what if we were to reframe our egos? When you make decisions to purchase a certain way, a discerning way—that is conscious living. It is not ego-based. It means that I am choosing to purchase this way because I have put certain standards in place. I believe it is better for me, my family, the people who produce these items, and the earth without doing harm. I won't eat fast food not because it is beneath me but because I am choosing healthier options. I am aware of the supply chain for the fast food world. I am aware of the factory farming crisis[39]

---

39   http://sites.psu.edu/elizabethnapolitanoci/2016/03/18/factory-farms-part-i/
http://sites.psu.edu/elizabethnapolitanoci/2016/03/30/factory-farming-part-ii/

and how these animals suffer. Even if I only had $5 to spend, it would be on raw vegetables and fruits.

For some reason, we seem to internalize others choices and believe they are affecting us personally. Maybe the real reason is because we are being a shown a different way of looking at life and the world and we are not ready to change. Even though we know it is better for all! We can always do better and elevate our choice to have a positive impact on this world. True luxury is a personal definition. It means something special to YOU. Luxury or status symbol, you choose.

Chapter 6

You Are What You Wear, Eat and Apply!

EMPOWER YOURSELF WITH A WELL-EQUIPPED TOOL BOX OF KNOWLEDGE!

"If you have accepted it, it won't change.
If you are thinking about it, you are open.
When you say NO MORE, change will happen."
— Tracey Martin

We have all heard it said before, "You are what you eat." Same goes for what you wear on your body and for what you put on your skin.

A correlation between fast food and fast fashion[40] has long been living in the same parallel universe in my mind and hopefully others as well. Everything we put in our mouths or on our skin becomes a part of our internal system, including toxic residue from the clothing we wear. Sometimes, it is easier for people to grasp the idea, "When I eat crap, I feel like crap." Your energy level is affected, your complexion, and your mental state—not to mention, your waistline! All of our personal care products have an effect on our bodies in some way.

WHO IS LOOKING OUT FOR YOU?

It has been a slow realization for us to wake up to the fact that the Environmental Protection Agency (EPA),[41] Food and Drug Administration (FDA),[42] and United States Department of Agriculture (USDA)[43] do not necessarily have our best interests at heart. So, it is up to each of us to make better choices. Spend your money with companies that are policing themselves. The

---

40   https://emilysfilms.wordpress.com/2016/09/23/fast-fashion-is-like-fast-food/
      http://www.huffingtonpost.in/entry/this-mother-went-a-whole-year-without-buying-clothes-for-her-family_us_57dc0c3ce4b0071a6e06d52a
41   http://www.foxnews.com/opinion/2017/01/17/sen-barrasso-for-8-years-epa-has-made-life-hard-for-too-many-americans-that-s-about-to-change.html
      https://www.theguardian.com/environment/2017/jul/20/epa-lawsuit-texas-industrial-air-pollution
42   https://www.wired.com/2015/02/infoporn-proof-fda-isnt-protecting-americans-health/
      http://www.naturalnews.com/2017-01-18-corruption-at-the-fda-is-to-blame-for-the-dramatic-increase-in-drugs-adverse-events-deaths.html#
43   http://wariscrime.com/new/top-10-most-useless-u-s-government-parasite-agencies/ (Check #3)
      http://thefederalist.com/2014/05/23/close-down-the-united-states-department-of-agriculture/

companies that just believe it is the right thing to do. Sustainable fashion and ethical practices should be accepted universally as good business practices.

We must reconnect with our minds, bodies, and spirits through the foods we eat, the clothing we wear, and the personal products we use.

The job of the sustainable fashion movement is to educate us and connect us back to ourselves, the planet, and each other. Go a little deeper. Why do you wear those great fitting jeans? How do they make you feel? What draws you to the styles you love? Shouldn't it be a multilayered process? The style should speak to you, as well as the fit, the way it is manufactured and the price. The bonus is how your clothes look on YOU! That is your own personal style. The hell with what *Vogue* or other powers that be say is "in" this year or what you should be purchasing. Sustainable fashion is more than thread deep. Gone are the days of scratchy hemp pants, baggy cotton t-shirts, and floppy Birkenstocks. (Although Birkenstocks are now making a BIG comeback!)

Creating sustainable fashion means slow fashion.[44] Sourcing ethical component and hardware companies, manufacturers, fabrics, dyes, laundry, artisans, and more takes time and a watchful vetting process. The supply chain can be a tricky one to follow. But it *can* and *is* being done. Respect what you wear and who makes it. It will make you feel great knowing the jeans that are hugging that bum of yours are doing good for the world, too.

---

44   https://www.notjustalabel.com/editorial/slow-fashion-movement

I am just going to put this out there. I believe the shift with fashion will happen quicker within the mindsets of customers than the shift to healthier eating has. It is two-fold. First, a lot of us are already in the consciousness that our food system needs to be reconstructed. Changing this part of our lives requires a lot of work. When I was training my clients full-time, I would lay out a food plan for them after meeting with their doctors and reviewing their blood work. This was a LONG process because it required each client to put in the work, and no one wants to work for it. But when your doctor tells you that you are one cheeseburger away from a heart attack, you are moved emotionally to get started. Secondly, with fashion, you are only required to purchase more mindfully and to think before you discard. You are going to buy clothing anyway; all I am asking you to do is ask thoughtful questions, look at the labels, shop locally when you can and THINK before you spend your money and don't waste it! That is pretty easy—you don't have to cut out the chocolate cake, work up a sweat or even forgo the appetizer at the next party.

Sustainability is a challenge, but I think we are all up for it! Don't just make it a checklist of items that you would LIKE to work on, instead make it a **Take Action** list that you will get done!

"If you are interested in something, you will look into a few things that you can change. If you are committed to changing, you will do whatever it takes!" — Tracey Martin

If you look at your life as a whole and want to make changes, it can be very overwhelming. I completely understand if you feel this way. However, when you compartmentalize the change, it becomes doable. Take one area at a time. Assess what it is you want to focus on for at least 21 days. Why 21 days? Because that is about how long it takes to change a behavior. The way you shop, eat, and what you wear are habits that can be broken and replaced with better choices. So, commit to not purchasing any new clothing for 21 days. Then maybe start with your daily personal hygiene products—look at the labels on all your skincare and makeup products. As you use them up, purchase better items that will meet your new set of standards. I have included a few of my favorites in the Chapter 9 resource section. No testing on animals, no chemicals, no fragrance or synthetic dyes. Use these as a guideline to get started. Draw your line in the sand!

Helpful tip: There is an app called EWG (Environmental Working Group)[45] that is a great tool to use to scan the product and investigate the ingredients in almost every skincare and makeup product on the market. But remember, once you know this information, you can't un-know it. I hope to be that nagging little voice in your head every time you head out on a shopping expedition or get online and start to tap the keys! I promise it will become habit after a while. You will begin to purchase more consciously. Be patient with yourself, but also hold yourself accountable. Maybe ask a friend to join you in this lifestyle evolution. The more, the merrier!

---

45   http://www.ewg.org/apps/

On our way to creating this change, language is so important. Educating ourselves on what is on a label and in our clothes is the first step to becoming aware. So, here is some basic terminology and lingo to look for on labels and hangtags, within social media content and on company websites.

Sustainability: Conserving an ecological balance by avoiding depletion of ANY natural resource.

*Defining **true sustainability** seems to be a personal thing, and it is important to note there are different levels of sustainability. My goal here is to create a clearer definition of what it means in general—to invite each person to try **sustainability** on for themselves. We need to meet the current needs of our world while preserving and mindfully thinking of our future generations.*

Conventionally Grown Cotton: Most of your clothing, household items, and bedding are made with conventionally grown cotton. This is the "dirtiest" cotton in the world, and the seeds have been genetically modified. They are sprayed with herbicides and pesticides—mostly with **Roundup**.[46] The primary ingredient in this compound is **glyphosate**.[47] It is a toxic chemical that is linked to cancer. The conventionally grown cotton fiber is also treated with chlorine bleach, ammonia, PFCs (Perfluorinated Chemicals), and VOCs as well as the deadly formaldehyde.

---

46 http://jech.bmj.com/content/early/2017/02/22/jech-2016-208463
   https://www.scientificamerican.com/article/weed-whacking-herbicide-p/
   https://www.ecowatch.com/15-health-problems-linked-to-monsantos-roundup-1882002128.html
   http://time.com/4711846/roundup-weed-killer-cancer/
47 http://npic.orst.edu/factsheets/glyphogen.html

VOC: Stands for Volatile Organic Compound. These materials are any compound of carbon, excluding carbon monoxide, carbon dioxide, carbonic acid, metallic carbides or carbonates and ammonium carbonate, which participates in atmospheric the photochemical reaction, except those designated by EPA as having negligible photochemical reactivity. *Yep, you guessed it, bad shit!*

Organic Cotton:[48] A cotton fiber grown according to the principles and requirements of the organic agriculture industry.

These rules are very strict and are defined by a law put in place by the European Union. Organic agriculture uses NO synthetic pesticides or fertilizers and NO genetically modified organisms. This label on any clothing item must be certified, transparent, and always traceable.

BT Cotton:[49] Cotton that has been genetically modified through a process that involves injecting it with one or more genes from common soil bacteria.

The bacteria then encode to produce insecticidal proteins that make the plants produce toxic chemicals as they grow.

Genetically Modified Organism (GMO):[50] An organism that has been altered by genetic engineering so that its DNA contains one or more genes that are not naturally occurring

---

48 https://www.cottonique.com/blogs/blog/8-benefits-of-organic-cotton-clothing

49 https://organic4greenlivings.com/gmo-cotton-the-ugly-facts/
http://www.greenpeace.org/international/en/news/features/adverse-impacts-of-ge-bt-cotto/

50 http://enhs.umn.edu/current/5103/gm/harmful.html
http://responsibletechnology.org/10-reasons-to-avoid-gmos/

If something is not made from organic cotton, you can bet it is a GMO! Here are a few examples of this process outside of the fashion industry, so you know how Frankensteinish this is:

1. *Strawberries and tomatoes are injected with fish genes from an Alaskan flounder[51] that can withstand arctic like temperatures to protect the fruit from freezing. The problem is, if we eat seasonal produce like we should, we won't have to worry about frozen fruit. I say no thank you to mutant fruit! By the way, this gene is attached to the fruit through a virus—more great news!*

2. *Salmon is injected with a growth hormone that allows it to continue to grow faster and shorten the waiting time for us...because it would be CRAZY to actually let nature take its course! It is the first genetically modified animal that is **allegedly** fit for human consumption. The American supermarket will be the first test market, so we should feel special, right? ...NOT! It is coming to the U.S. first because most other countries have completely outlawed the use of GMOs.[52]*

3. *Dairy cows are injected with genetically modified hormones (rBGH and rBST)[53] to increase milk production. This is*

---

51 http://www.motherearthnews.com/real-food/adding-a-fish-gene-into-tomatoes-zmaz00amzgoe

52 http://www.collective-evolution.com/2015/10/07/heres-why-19-countries-in-europe-just-completely-banned-genetically-modified-crops/

http://nutritionstudies.org/gmo-dangers-facts-you-need-to-know/

53 https://www.cancer.org/cancer/cancer-causes/recombinant-bovine-growth-hormone.html

http://www.huffingtonpost.com/samuel-s-epstein/the-dangers-of-geneticall_b_633955.html

only one atrocity that is committed against the dairy cow. Because they only produce milk when they are pregnant, they are raped repeatedly with bull semen right after giving birth to their calves so that they can continue to produce milk at unnatural rates. Meanwhile, their calves are taken away (because we wouldn't want them drinking "our" milk). They are confined in tiny crates for 6 months and then slaughtered for veal. Cow's milk should only be for baby cows!

Fair Trade Certified: A trading partnership based on dialogue, transparency, and respect that seeks greater equality in international trade.

It contributes to sustainable development by offering better trading conditions and securing the rights of marginalized producers and workers. There are rigorous social, environmental, and economic standards put into place to ensure these parameters are followed. When you choose products with the Fair Trade label on them, your day-to-day purchases can improve an individual's life, as well as improving entire communities and creating change within the industry.

Sweatshop:[54] An unpleasant and dangerous place to work within the fashion industry's supply chain.

Workers include both adults and children as young as eight years old working on as little as $2 a day in very poor conditions.

---

54 http://www.dailymail.co.uk/news/article-3339578/Crammed-squalid-factories-produce-clothes-West-just-20p-day-children-forced-work-horrific-unregulated-workshops-Bangladesh.html
http://www.publicseminar.org/2016/01/global-sweatshops-solidarity-and-the-bangladesh-breakthrough/#.WaG3gz4jGM8

These facilities are poorly regulated, if at all. The environment and the workers' welfare are not taken into consideration at all.

Low-Impact Dye: A dye that has been classified by a certification process called Oeko-Tex Standard.

These dyes still contain chemicals; however, they are classified as not containing "harsh chemicals." They require less rinsing and have a high absorption rate in the fabric.

Oeko-Tex Standard 100: An international certification process

It is an independent testing certification system for the textile industry and products in all stages of production along the textile value supply chain. This certification system focuses on the toxic chemicals and additives that are present during the manufacturing process.

GOTS (Global Organic Textile Standards) Certification:[55] An international certification for fabrics, yarn and clothing that meet a variety of criteria covering the production, processing, manufacturing, packaging, labeling, exportation, importation, and distribution of all-natural fibers. GOTS has taken things further than other certifications by including the source of the fiber and all components of production.

It is considered a very trustworthy label and has undergone four revisions to date. Most ethical companies who are certified should display this certification, or at least the approved seal on their website.

REACH Certification: This stands for Registration, Evaluation, Authorization, and Restriction of Chemicals. Put in place

---

55 http://www.global-standard.org/

due to regulations by the European Union to improve protection of human health and the environment as pertaining to the textile and garment industries.

BLUESIGN Certification: Bluesign, founded in 2000, is a global partner for a sustainable textile industry.

It eliminates harmful substances right from the beginning of the manufacturing process and sets and controls standards for environmentally friendly and safe production.

Global Recycled Standard (GRC): A product standard for tracking and verifying the content of recycled materials in a final product, while ensuring strict production requirements.

Cradle to Cradle (C2C): Products are assessed in five different categories: Material Health, Reutilization, Renewable Energy/Carbon Management, Water Stewardship, and Social Fairness. C2C suggests that industry must protect and enrich ecosystems and nature's biological metabolism while also maintaining a safe, productive technical metabolism for high-quality use and circulation of organic and technical nutrients. It is a holistic economic, industrial, and social form of work that seeks to create systems that are not only efficient but also essentially waste free.

This standard is meant to guide designers and manufacturers through a continual improvement process encompassing the above categories.

B-Corp Business: Stands for Benefit Corporation. This type of US based business entity is growing a large following. It means that it is a for-profit business with a focus on positive impacts in society, on employees, the community, and environment. A quadruple bottom line!

Eco-Fashion: Clothing and other goods made from recycled materials or otherwise produced by methods that are not harmful to the environment, human beings, animals, and the ecosystem.

This beautiful word came into being due to the vision of a fashion pioneer named Marci Zaroff.

Cruelty Free Fashion: If you see this label on products that you use, it means that the company does not engage in testing, harming or killing animals during the production or manufacturing of its products. For cosmetics, it also encompasses the testing on animals which is violent and cruel and most of the times ends in the death of the animal. On your cosmetic label, look for the leaping bunny logo. *Download the free leaping bunny app on your Smartphone to keep you in the know!*

Plant Based Fashion: This is a very small but growing category. It indicates that every level of production and manufacturing are derived from plants. The fibers, yarns, dyeing process, and finished garment have zero byproduct of anything other than plants. Plant-based fashion is also vegan. However, vegan is not always plant based. More on that below. Think clothing made with linen, tencel, organic cotton, hemp, and bamboo.

Vegan Fashion: This one is kind of a mixed message. No animals were used to make the fashion. However, most of the components are chemical based. PVC (poly vinyl chloride) is vegan but not environmentally or humanity friendly. Forms of plastics, acrylic, and PU (poly urethane) and polyester (made from crude oil) are all considered vegan, but it stops there! Read the labels.

Capsule Collection: This term refers to a small collection of essential basics that will remain relevant despite the fickleness of the fashion industry and the customer.

Circular Economy: This is an alternative way of thinking within the sphere of *economics*. A traditional economy is considered *linear* which can be defined as make, use, and dispose. Circular economy is the revolutionary way of thinking. To keep our resources in use as long as possible, using them to the maximum value, then recover and regenerate products and materials at the end of each service life.

Ethical Fashion: An *umbrella* term that covers the design, manufacturing, sourcing, and selling of a product.

It is also meant to cover the working conditions of the employees, Fair Trade, sustainable production, and animal rights/welfare.

Fiber: Okay, we are not talking about the dietary fiber here. We are talking about fiber in fashion. Fiber is the filament that is made from vegetable, plant, or mineral substance to form a textile.

Yarn: Yarn is spun threads that are created from the fibers to be woven together, sewn or knitted to create a fabric or textile for the fashion industry.

Artisan-Made: An item made by hand using traditional methods by a person skilled in a particular art or craft. These skills are usually passed down from generation to generation as well as culturally.

Buy Local: Shopping at local Farmers markets, boutiques (carrying sustainable fashion lines of course!), and small businesses to support your community

One of the BEST practices you can put into play! Shopping local ensures your purchases have a contained carbon footprint.

Eco-Lux: Luxury products that are good for the planet.

Eco means having to do with the environment and environmentally-friendly goods, services, laws, guidelines, and policies put in place to protect against anything harming our ecosystem. Lux refers to a luxury or overall high standard of living or lifestyle. Put these two terms together and you get one of my favorite new words that is finally gaining more momentum. These two terms were not always used to together until recently. Normally, luxury meant "excessive consumption" or producing something at "all costs" for a discerning wealthy clientele. Today, we are moving away from this mindset and the old definition. We are in the process of redefining luxury to mean local, handmade, one-of-a-kind or unique. People want to know where, how and by whom their products were made. Luxury today has substance and a conscience. It is not pretentious or snobby. The REAL VALUE is in the beauty and the story behind the product and company.

Transparency: This means there is a commitment by the company to publish its total impact in manufacturing throughout its supply chain. Transparency includes a company's policies, raw materials, processing facilities, dyeing, printing, finishing, and final stage production. It encompasses their practices, social, and environmental impact while having special focus on the workers. Plain and simple—when companies are not transparent, it will cost lives. Brands must visit every aspect of their supply chain first hand and then make it available so positive changes can be made.

This information is communicated to the public, staff, share-holders, and all persons in the supply chain, and includes the dyeing of the fabric and the growing of the fibers. It also takes into account the non-renewable resources that were used and any animal byproducts.

<u>Note:</u> Currently there is a movement within the industry to publish list of suppliers along the supply chain. Fashion Revolution has implemented a Fashion Transparency Index so this can be measured and made public.

Traceability: Companies that can verify the place of origin, location, and sourcing of all components required in the production of their goods and services.

Traceability along the entire supply chain from workers to buyers and sellers of goods should be available through transparent business practices.

Carbon-Neutral Footprint: Achieving net zero carbon emissions by balancing a measured amount of carbon released with an equivalent amount offset.

Sounds complicated but it actually isn't. For example, if you carpool, you are a carbon neutral commuter.

Fast Fashion:[56] To fast track looks from the runway to the clothing rack to your closet.

This is the buzz word of the day. Although it was put in use around the mid-90s, brands were looking for ways to increase

---

56   http://www.thefashionlaw.com/learn/fast-fashions-green-initiatives-dont-believe-the-hype

profits. The focus is put on the source supply chain to ensure quick delivery, cheap fabrics, and cheap labor—all so that customers can buy what they just saw on the runway faster. This method is typically used by large chains like Topshop, Primark, Zara, H&M, and Forever21. A typical time frame is two weeks from production to the store shelf, which is an impossible feat in the normal production calendar. It has disrupted the traditional fashion cycle of manufacturing and not for the better.

Carcinogen:[57] A substance found in many foods, textiles sprayed with pesticides, synthetically-dyed makeup, personal care items, clothing, and home products.

Carcinogens are capable of causing cancer in living tissue. This substance can enter our bodies through respiratory pathways, absorption into the epidermis, or ingestion. It can alter our DNA on a cellular level.

Formaldehyde:[58] A smelly, colorless gas made by oxidizing methanol that is used to embalm the deceased.

It is often sprayed inside the containers coming from overseas that are packed with your clothing. It is typically used on fabrics that crease easily and mildew during transport. If your clothing is wrinkle-resistant, it has a formaldehyde-based resin in the fabric. More on this in Chapter 8.

Heavy Metals: Lead, cadmium, and mercury—highly toxic natural compounds that are used in certain dyes and pigments.

---

57 https://www.ncbi.nlm.nih.gov/pmc/articles/PMC4986180/
    http://toxicfashion.org/chemical-txtugly.html
58 https://www.cottonique.com/blogs/blog/7-reasons-why-formaldehyde-in-clothing-is-dangerous-and-how-to-protect-yourself

These metals can be absorbed through the body and can build up to toxic levels with some effects being irreversible. They can damage the nervous system, liver, and kidneys and have also been linked to cancer.

Chromium:[59] A substance used in the tanning of leather

Eighty to 95 percent of all consumable leather is tanned with chromium. When toxic levels of this compound are found in the body, the results are devastating—not only for the person wearing it but also for the workers producing the leather. Workers who are inhaling this substance can develop lung and sinus cancers, along with a host of other respiratory issues. Customers wearing the products can develop dermatitis, auto immune disorders or other mysterious illnesses.

Note: *PG&E dumped roughly 370 million gallons of chromium and tainted the groundwater in Hinkley, CA. You might remember this incident since it is the premise of the Erin Brockovich movie. PG&E paid $333 Million in a settlement to the residents suffering from the effects of this heinous act.*

Greenwashing: Ahh! Everything is all about perception. This term refers to a certain way of crafting or spinning a language to make the customer believe that they are doing good with their purchase. They, the company that you are purchasing from is doing things with a conscious mind and in an environmentally-friendly way. Be on the lookout!

Data and definitions found and received from: Wikipedia, Green Peace Detox Fashion campaign, and American Chemical Society.

---

59 http://gizmodo.com/how-leather-is-slowly-killing-the-people-and-places-tha-1572678618

THE NOT-SO FRIENDLY SKIES. A SEVERE WARDROBE MALFUNCTION AND LESSONS IN TOXICITY.

A few months back, I was on an American Airlines[60] flight. I commented to the flight attendant about their new uniforms.

She began to inform me of the virtual nightmare that the flight attendants and some pilots and even passengers had been going through. Why you might ask? Well, it was their uniforms. Yes, the garments that they wear every day and are required for their jobs.

The employees were dealing with unexplainable rashes, severe skin reactions, and respiratory conditions that were sending some of them to the emergency room. Passengers on some flights had even experienced bloody noses.

After hearing this from the attendant, I knew without a doubt that it was the reaction of the fibers that were used to make the uniforms, the chemical dyes, and the toxic chemicals used to finish them and make them "wrinkle resistant"—all heavy metals.

According to the union, the Association of Professional Flight Attendants, over 3470 employees have reported issues. The airlines have still not issued a total recall of the uniforms.[61] This

---

60 http://www.chicagotribune.com/business/ct-american-airlines-flight-attendant-uniforms-20170118-story.html
http://www.star-telegram.com/news/business/aviation/sky-talk-blog/article142064664.html
https://www.usatoday.com/story/travel/flights/todayinthesky/2017/06/21/american-airlines-seek-new-uniform-maker-after-illness-complaints/416925001/

61 https://www.dallasnews.com/business/american-airlines/2017/06/14/american-airlines-still-searching-long-term-solution-problem-uniforms-ceo-doug-parker-says
https://www.dallasnews.com/business/american-airlines/2017/01/24/four-tests-2600-complaints-later-american-airlines-flight-attendants-still-reporting-uniform-problems

brings up another issue. Where will they dispose of these "hazardous material" uniforms? America Airlines and Twin Hill (the manufacturer) have said that they have done all the mandatory testing and the levels of these toxic chemicals were found to be within the "acceptable" range. Is there really an "acceptable range" for toxic chemicals? Our immune systems are already compromised with the amount of **toxins** that we live with on a daily basis. Shouldn't we be mindful and lessen the load when possible? I believe a third party entity needs to conduct independent studies on the uniforms. Additionally, American Airlines needs to support the grievances of their employees. After all, they are the company's greatest natural resource. Their people!

This issue is something that we all must think about. It is not just the uniforms that are used by Aviation employees. Any uniform that can't be laundered and needs to be dry cleaned (organically) is most likely manufactured in the same way. Because the uniforms are created to be wrinkle resistant, they will never see the inside of your washer and dryer. This is the problem. When I think of where else these problems might begin to surface, I think of band uniforms of high school or college students and other institutions that require these types of uniforms to be worn.

Before making your purchase, be in the know and always be willing to take a few extra minutes and read the labels of your clothing. It will empower you and enable you to make more informed decisions. Go FORTH and educate yourself!

Chapter 7

Awareness and Action for Change

The first step is to become more mindful of your own shopping and purchasing habits. What triggers you to go shopping? Is it the need to stock up on a few basic items, or is shopping often just an excuse to have a fun time out when you're stressed, depressed or bored? Next time you see a sale sign as you're driving by a store, think twice before swerving your car into oncoming traffic to make that last-minute turn into the parking lot. Just because something is on sale doesn't mean: a) you need it or b) you need to buy it. Take inventory of your closet before you hit the mall to determine what you actually need or need to replace. Organize your clothes into sections: Shop, Keep, Consign, Redesign, Donate, and Recycle.

SHOP (YOUR OWN CLOSET)

Sometimes, the best finds are already in your own closest! Humans tend to be creatures of habit, and this behavior kicks in when we open our closets and look straight ahead. Since we only see about four feet directly in front of us, anything lurking on the outer edges of our closet often gets lost. In fact, we even put the clean clothes away right in the center. Next time you do laundry, try something different. After wearing and washing your clothes, put them to the far right, so your unworn clothes have a chance to work their way to the center. Eventually, a treasure trove of new clothes you completely forgot about will magically reappear. Have fun combining and trying on the "new" old stuff to see what you can create. Do this until you work your way through your entire closet and rediscover some great things!

__Tip:__ Sometimes, it is not the actual garment you don't like but the way it fits you. Take it to a good seamstress and ask them to make the specific fit changes. It will make a huge difference.

KEEP

This is an extremely personal section. Only you know what you love and don't want to part with. However, these few helpful hits may make it easier for you to decide:

1. If you haven't worn something in two years or more, like the song says, "Let it goooo!" This is a typical time-frame to use as a guide. We tend to push things aside that never make it back into the rotation, and before

you know it, a couple of years have passed, and it needs to go!

2. Classics to keep are anything made from cashmere (good cashmere), wool, cotton, silk or natural fibers—these have lasting power. A beautiful wool blazer will always serve you well, as will a great fitting pair of jeans that never go out of style. Even a basic little black dress is always a keeper, or an amazing silk scarf. These pieces are timeless, and you can work with them to create updated styles just by combining pieces or adding a few accessories to them.

3. If you have some fun pieces that "define the current decade," keep them! I wish I would have done this. I could have saved myself lots of cash, as my girls are loving the 90s comeback looks and they love shopping vintage and thrift! I find myself buying some of the same styles that I once wore—only now they are cool! Ugh!

CONSIGN

When it comes to consignment stores, there have been some interesting things popping up lately! Here's how this process works: After going through your closet and finding things that still have lots of life left in them but are no longer your style, find a consignment store in your area. Bag the clothing up and drop it off in good condition, making organically dry clean items as needed. *(Tip: It will mean more green in your pocket if you take the time to care for them.)* The store will then open an account in your name, and once your items sell, you will have a credit worth cold hard cash. Sometimes, they will even offer you store credit that is up to 20% more than the cash option to buy some new threads. Consignment stores offer a range of items from high-end luxury to great finds for teens. Or, if online shopping is more your style, these apps are FAST, EASY and FUN:

Poshmark – This site features more of the high-end designer items. Just take great photos of your clothing item and upload them to your account through the free app. Once your item sells, you will be notified via email. They will send you a prepaid printed label that makes it easy to package up your item, slap the label on it, and send it off! Include a nice thank you card for a more personalized touch and to encourage repeat business. Once the purchaser receives their item, they will enter their app and press "accept." Once this is done, the money will be deposited into your account. This is a great way to make some serious extra cash. A friend of mine made about $10,000 in a few months selling some desirable designer items. If you build up a following and receive good ratings, you can grow a lovely little side business for yourself.

Website: www.poshmark.com

Depop/Mercari – These two apps feature more mid-priced items and are perfect for teens and 20-somethings. The process for both is similar to Poshmark's, except when it comes to shipping, you have to head to the post office and do it the old-fashioned way. My girls have done well selling their things here and purchasing some cool clothes. And it's not just limited to apparel. You can find shoes, vintage records, and fun bedroom accessories as well!

Websites: www.depop.com

www.mercari.com

Other notable apps include:

Let Go www.letgo.com

ThredUp www.thredup.com

Vinted www.vinted.com

Tradesy www.tradesy.com

VarageSale www.varagesale.com

Ebay www.ebay.com

Closet 5 www.closet5.com

The best part of shopping consignment and resale is there is no need for more clothing to be manufactured. This extends the life of the clothing and keeps it going. There is so much excess in the fashion world—this is an easy way to help keep the balance! You can follow some of your favorite celebrities and fashion models on these apps as well. They put online "stores" up selling pieces from their wardrobe and usually the money is donated to their favorite charity.

REDESIGN

If you love an item but its style factor is past its prime, try redesigning it to create a new look. The easiest redesign project is taking your favorite pair of holey, worn-out jeans and cutting them to make a timeless pair of shorts. Another great idea is to grab some cute fabric and sew it on the inside of your jeans so when you put them on, you no longer see skin, only the cute fabric peeking out of the holes. Even dress pants can be cut and made into a trendy pair of dress shorts. When it comes to old jean jackets, grab some fun iron-on appliqués and give your jacket a new look. Old dress? Cut it in half and make the bottom into an adorable skirt. Take a dress shirt and turn it into a short-sleeved blouse. Even a blazer can be fun without the sleeves! T-shirts can be made into great little mini dresses or even bikinis.

If sewing is not YOUR thing, find a talented tailor or seamstress to help with your clothing transformations. Visit Pinterest to get your creative juices flowing and have fun! Look online for your local city phone directory, and you will find resources for all of these talented people. Let's keep them busy!

DONATE

Let's face it. Donating something to someone in need makes us feel good! We go through our closet, bag up our old clothes and drop them off at the nearest Goodwill or Red Cross location. While this is a generous deed, sometimes it unfortunately causes more harm than good. If these thrift stores can't sell the goods, they get bundled up and discounted. Then if they still do not sell, they are shipped off to other countries. In the wake of a disaster, this is a good thing. But when these items keep stacking up, they become nothing more than a toxic garbage pile. Think before you donate. If possible, try to find a local family or shelter you can take your items to where they will be put to immediate use. One more thought is, set up a shop on one of the above apps and sell your clothing there with the proceeds going to a worthy charity. What a great way to pay it forward!

RECYCLE

Did you know EACH one of us throws away about 62 pounds of clothing a year? These items end up in landfills, and due to the toxicity of the fabrics, dyes, and finishes it takes to produce our clothes, the discarded apparel gives off methane gas, which is a chemical compound 20 times more effective at trapping heat than its infamous counterpart, carbon dioxide. Methane is one of the most potent greenhouse gases contributing to global warming, and its other major cause outside of the fashion industry lies in animal agriculture. Yes, cow poop, burps, and farts give off massive amounts of methane gas, but that is a whole other story! Recycling your clothing and home goods is one of the best things you can do; they won't end up in a landfill or pollute our environment.

NOTE: Just because you can recycle, it doesn't mean you should purchase more clothing. It is still always best to buy less!

Most city government websites have a list of textile recycling centers in your area. If not, you can sponsor one! A bin will be dropped off at your specified work or school location and is serviced once a month. Be sure to work with a company that is transparent about their recycling practices. Below are some of the recycling companies that offer this service. Check the websites to see if they are available in your area. If not, do a quick Google search, and you should be able to find similar companies. As a society, we have gotten used to recycling our plastic, glass and paper products. Now, it is time to do the same with our clothing, bedding, towels, linens, and shoes.

RECYCLING COMPANIES

1. Planet Aid (www.planetaid.org)

This company believes that reusing clothing and reducing the need for manufacturing new clothes is an easy way to save resources and mitigate climate change. Planet Aid collects and recycles 100 million pounds of clothes and shoes every year, but that is just a fraction of the textiles that could be recycled if everyone stopped throwing their clothes in the trash.

2. American Textile Recycling Services (ATRS) (www.atrscorp.com)

This company believes that textile recycling should be easily accessible to all. That's the reason they have placed thousands of donation bins in neighborhoods across the United States. This company is committed to keeping textiles out of landfills, cleaning up the local communities, and creating a greener tomorrow for generations to come. You'll find their professionally maintained donation bins at shopping centers, major malls, local groceries, convenience and drug store parking lots.

3. Secondary Materials and Recycled Textiles (SMART) (www.smartasn.org)

This company is committed to educating the public on the benefits of clothing and textile recycling and the impact diverting these materials will have on the nation's landfills. SMART aims to attain their goal of zero clothing and textiles going into landfills by 2037. This company strives to promote interaction among those involved in all aspects of clothing including consumers, manufacturers, retailers, municipalities, and recyclers.

Also, this company is developing a resource library of clothing and textile recycling information.

4. USA GAIN (www.usagain.com)

This company believes everything can be **used again**. They work to reduce textile waste by providing thousands of convenient locations across the U.S. where you can recycle textiles any time of the day and any day of the year. Check out the ticker on their website showing how many cubic yards of landfill was saved by using their services.

5. Phoenix Fibers (phxfibers.com)

This company does a fiber conversion program that is so awesome! They convert over 300 tons of denim and other cotton fabric into fibers to create a product called **Ultratouch**, which is a denim insulation used in homes and businesses, for appliance and auto insulation, and is even used to make prison mattresses. Now that is a great use of waste! There are companies like this all over the world.

HOW ABOUT A GOOD OLE' FASHIONED DETOX?

Even if you do go through your closet and consign, donate or recycle a few items to free up some space, try committing to not shopping for a specified amount of time. There is a beautiful word in the English language we all need to start putting into practice more often ...NO! There's no reason you can't make do with what you have for a while, and if you do need something, borrow it! This is such a freeing exercise because, let's face it, we all have a closet that could clothe a small village.

Instead of spending the day shopping, adopt a different hobby to fill your idle time. And when you get those coupon flyers in the mail tempting you, throw them in the recycling bin. If you want to take it to the extreme, unsubscribe from all store and brand emails. Bye-bye (pun intended) inbox temptations! And don't forget to ignore the algorithm monster that tracks your every move. Click on that innocent looking image of a super cute sweater, and it will haunt you until you cave in and purchase it. Don't buy, click or share any kind of clothing items during this time. Be strong! You got this. Email me if you need support! sustainableinstilettos@gmail.com

Now that you've freed up some space in your closet and made it through the Detox period, here are some sustainable ways to replace the items you need:

1. **Make a shopping ~~lust~~ (oops) list**

   Be smart and arm yourself with a detailed shopping list. I'm sure you make a grocery list before going to the market, so why not approach your clothing shopping the same way?

   Normcore[62] is a great way to dress and shop. Norm, as I'm sure you guessed, stands for "normal," and "core" stands for "hardcore." Normcore essentially means dressing in a way that is authentic to you but doing it, so you are not distinguishing yourself from others just

---

62 https://www.popsugar.com/fashion/How-Wear-Normcore-Trend-35991288
    https://www.thecut.com/2014/09/14-normcore-street-style-looks from-fashion-week/slideshow/2014/09/11/street_style_bestdressednyfwday7/

through your clothing and labels. The key is to buy ethical, well-made, stylish clothing pieces that are timeless. Think about an outfit consisting of an amazing pair of denim jeans and a favorite sexy, organic V-neck tee paired with a badass vintage leather jacket. Finish the look off with a pair of vegan leather stilettos and your favorite bag, and there you have it—Normcore!

For days spent at home relaxing, grab a cardigan with that "lived-in" feel you love so much and a pair of roomy track pants, and lounging just got kicked up a notch! You get the idea. Make a list of things you truly need and will wear repeatedly. And always make each look your own! Take some photos of your favorite fashions and keep them in an album on your phone so you can recreate the looks you love.

__Hint:__ This is a great idea for kids and teens who have a hard time figuring out what to wear every day to school. Take photos and name the albums. This seriously helps to save time and arguments in the morning. A little peace in the morning before school is always a good thing.

2. **Viva la vintage!**

Oh, how I love vintage clothing shopping! It is seriously a treasure hunt through time. Each decade is defined by its fashion, so digging through clothing from different eras is truly a history lesson in and of itself. You can spot an outfit and know exactly what decade it came from, and the feeling and craftsmanship from clothing made in past decades is incomparable. You can also be sure that when you purchase something vintage, no one else will be wearing it. Shopping vintage ensures your clothes have another life.

Here are a few helpful hints from one of the best vintage collectors in the market today, Misty Guerriero, owner of Vintage by Misty.

Why Should We Purchase Vintage Over New?

A quality vintage garment or accessory can cost as much as a current piece of contemporary fashion (ahem, vintage Chanel), so why would someone choose a pre-owned item over something brand new? It's hands down made better. "A general rule of thumb, especially for higher-end designer pieces, is that the older the piece, the higher the quality."

Where to Purchase Quality Vintage

"Vintage denotes something special—that an item has stood the test of time and has remained relevant for any number of reasons—timelessness of style, quality, historical or cultural significance or interesting provenance." Look in your local high-end vintage shops or in major cities and seek out vintage markets that have dealers from all over the world. Another way is to visit cities that have a history. You're definitely going to find shops that seek out quality.

Not All Vintage is Good Vintage

You may fall in love with a beautiful printed garment or a beaded dress, but check to see if the fabric is in good condition. "I always like to really look at and touch the clothing, to make sure it still has life in it. Vintage pieces often get brittle and dry and shatter. There's nothing more heartbreaking than investing some money in something and having it fall apart on you. If a garment looks like it's cracking, pulling, falling apart, or fading, it's probably wise to leave it where you found it."

Find An Era You Love, Then Find Designers From That Era

"Typically, the easiest eras to shop would be the ones closest to now, so think early 90s... designers like Versace, Chanel, Issey Miyake, Escada, and McQueen were on top of their game. In the 80s, you had designers like Christian Lacroix, Moschino, Levi's, Thierry Mugler, and Judith Leiber, to name a few. In the 70s, fashion took a huge turn, and you had designers like Yves Saint Laurent, Givenchy, Gottex, Thea Porter, and Missoni putting their mark on the fashion scene. In the 60s, it was all mod (think Twiggy and Andy Warhol); you had designers like Pucci, Pierre Cardin, Gucci, and Hermes. The easiest eras to fit into a contemporary wardrobe would be those from the latter half of the 20th century (1960s onward). Items from before that might be considered too costume-y if not incorporated well into your personal style."

Travel to Hunt

I love traveling to countries where there are major fashion houses, like London, Milan, Paris or even Tel Aviv! You'll find so many unique vintage pieces, both non-designer and designer. Purchase what inspires you. That's what makes fashion so much fun!

To experience this beautiful store, and find out more about Misty visit: www.vintagebymisty.com.

We had to get another perspective on vintage because we LOVE it so much! Here is a mini interview from the one and only Mr. Robert Black of **Fashion by Robert Black**.

Robert is a vintage fashion aficionado. He travels the world in search of the clothing to bring a whole new vintage experience to red carpet couture, special occasion designer pieces, dynamic daywear, exceptional accessories, and historic treasures all in like new condition.

SIS: What decade in fashion do you believe has the most craftsmanship within its designs?

Robert: For me, the 1940s have the most interesting and architectural designs. People had less because of the war; however, I believe that made them far more creative!

SIS: Who is your all-time fave designer?

Robert: I personally love William Travilla. He was one of the Hollywood Golden Boys. His career included designing Marilyn Monroe's white dress (the most expensive dress ever sold in auction), and his ready-to-wear always had a bit of the movie star glamour built in.

SIS: Can you give us 5 tips to finding great vintage?
Robert:

1. Don't judge a book by its cover, as many items do not have hanger appeal. But back then, they knew how to fit a woman's figure.

2. Don't be afraid to try something out of your box. That is the fun of vintage shopping!

3. Buy quality versus quantity.

4. See what's hanging in your mother's/grandmother's/ aunt's closet. They were young and hot once, too!

5. Look for vintage shops when you travel; great items pop up everywhere.

SIS: What got you interested in curating vintage?

Robert: History, preservation, and art....fashion is art!

SIS: What is your perspective on the current condition of the fashion industry as a whole?

Robert: I am always amazed looking through the major fashion magazines and collections to see how much today's designers literally copy (are not inspired by, but *copy*) the past. I love a designer who has a new fashion perspective and is not afraid to show it!

To find out more about Robert,

visit: www.fashionbyrobertblack.com.

RENT THE DESIGNER

For a special event, my go-to website is www.renttherunway. com. You can rent the most gorgeous designer dress for a spectacular night out on the town, and return it the next day. Just get it organically dry cleaned and ship it back—easy as that! And often the whole process costs under $100. Through this service, you can honor the fashion industry in a mindful way. A woman I know even outfitted all her bridesmaids with dresses from here, which makes so much sense considering no one EVER wears a bridesmaid dress again.

Can you maintain this sustainable way of life? Yes, you can! Choosing to live a more sustainable way of life means choosing to be mindful of others and the planet. There are two things most of us do every morning without thought: 1) We get dressed, and 2) We eat breakfast. We may not realize it, but these things affect millions of people all around the world. Someone picked those berries you are enjoying for breakfast. (Usually while bending over for hours in the sweltering sun for nothing more than migrant worker wages.) And someone else grew the fibers that were harvested, cleaned, milled, and made into the yarn that was then woven into the fabric to make your t-shirt. Learn to take a moment out of each day to reflect and be grateful for these things we so often take for granted. Value the clothing you wear and take care of it. Your clothing should last and work for you.

When I speak to groups, one of the most frequently asked questions is, "Now that I know this information, where can I shop?" It is always important to do your homework on brands before you buy. Wait...I already did it for you! Chapter 9 has a list of over 100 websites and resources, what they sell and how they do business. This is meant to inform you and empower you to go forth and shop mindfully!

Chapter 8

Garment Care 101 and Beyond

CINDERELLA'S GOT NOTHING ON US!

We all know that to make things last, we need to care for them properly. I can remember my mom telling me on the first day of school, "Don't drag your feet and scuff up your new shoes; they need to last all year!" Well, if I REALLY liked my shoes, I listened. But if I didn't, the first thing I did was jump on the swings and drag my feet every time I went back and forth, slowly wearing down the sole just so I could get a new pair. Sorry, Mom! I'm sure you already knew that!

When we are first learning how to do laundry, we learn that reds don't go with whites and darks need to be washed separately. In my house, this is a BIG deal! Once my girls turn 13, I do not do their laundry any longer; it is up to them. However, I won't let them do mine either. Otherwise, my whites would be gray. Oh, and bleach...forget about it! My point is, just like my girls,

you might not be caring for your clothes the way you should—the green way. There is a whole new set of laundry rules to learn aside from the basic stuff.

RULES OF WASHING

First of all, ALWAYS wash your clothes before you wear anything! You never know the path it has taken before it made its way into your closet.

Are you washing your clothes too often? Are you reading the instruction labels?

1. One simple thing to start with is the temperature. Are you still washing your whites in hot water? Yikes! Change the temperature! Washing in warm or cold is so much better for your clothing, as well as your energy bill. According to my washing machine instructions, I could save almost $60 a year just by lowering the water temperature. Most of the energy used to wash your clothes is just to produce the hot water. Also, a lot of natural fibers, cotton, silks, and hemp are dyed, so when you wash clothes in cold water, it will preserve their color longer. These fibers are strong but can succumb to hot temperatures that cause them to fray, break, and show wear sooner. The whole idea is to make clothing last after we have taken the time and spent the money to invest in the good stuff.

For denim jeans, wear them at least 10 times before you wash them. Between wearings, put them in a bag and in the freezer to kill any germs and refresh the smell. Seriously, this works! Denim is a hardy fabric, and the more you wear and less you wash it, the better the fit will be. The color will fade evenly, and they will last longer. Try it!

2. If you have the space, get an air dryer or a small clothesline outside. Have you smelled freshly washed laundry hanging from a clothesline lately? It smells so amazing! Clothes break down faster in the dryer; they shrink and they can even bleed onto other garments. And taking into consideration energy...you'll save more, too! Don't forget, this cuts down on the emission of greenhouse gases as well. Even in the winter, use the air dryer and just put it somewhere in your house. With your heater running, the clothes get dry faster and still smell good. If they feel a little stiff, just run them through the dryer for 10 minutes on the "fluff" cycle. This does the trick. Dry sweaters and delicates flat so they keep their shape.

3. What products should I use to wash my clothes? I get this question all the time. I have lots of answers. A fun thing to do is to make your own detergent. If you have kids, they totally get into this. Promise, it is simple and saves you money. Here is the recipe:

    a. Baking soda: 1½ cups

b. Washing soda (you can find this at any supermarket): 1½ cups

c. Natural soap (I use Dr. Bronner's. I am in with love their entire line!) Get a bar of it and grate it into the measuring cup: ¾ cup

d. Lavender essential oil: 40 drops

Combine all of this with 2 gallons of water and mix well. Store it in an air-tight container. For each load, use about 2 TBS of detergent. While the washing machine is filling up, sprinkle the detergent in with the water stream.

When it comes to softening your clothes, try this:

White vinegar: 6 cups

Baking soda: 1 cup

Lemon or lavender essential oil: 20 drops

Mix the vinegar and oil together, then stir in the baking soda. It will fizz and bubble a bit. Once it has calmed down, put it into a large, air-tight container. Use about 3/4 of a cup per load. You can add this to your rinse cycle or put it into the softener compartment. See if this makes your clothes soft and static-free. If not, increase the amount a bit next time.

If you are not the DIY type, I totally understand! Here are some great brands to look for. Some are even Cradle 2 Cradle certified. (If you can't remember what that is, flip back to Chapter 6.)

1. Biokleen Laundry Liquid

2. Seventh Generation

3. Ecos Laundry

4. Whole Foods 365 Brand

5. Method Brand 8X Laundry detergent

6. Mrs. Meyers brand

7. Molly's Suds

Of course, if you can buy these brands in their recycled containers, please do. Some come in biodegradable packaging as well. It gets better and better!

Fun Tip: **To get rid of static, save all your aluminum foil and then make it into a ball about the size of a tennis ball. Throw it in the dryer with your clothes. This will help fight static while softening your clothes. It should last about 35 loads. Imagine all the chemicals you are saving yourself and your family from!**

Fast Fact: **Americans spend 7 Billion dollars on dry cleaning each year.**

By the way, dry cleaning is not **dry**. If you must dry clean something, dry "green" it instead! The regular dry cleaning process is extremely toxic. They use a nasty liquid solvent chemical called perchloroethylene, or perc[63] for short. This chemical is considered to be a neurological toxin and an environmental pollutant by the EPA. This means it has known or suspected properties that cause cancer and other serious health effects. Imagine the people working with this chemical every day... breathing it in over long periods of time can cause liver and kidney damage. As customers, we bring our garments home in

---

63 https://toxtown.nlm.nih.gov/text_version/chemicals.php?id=22

plastic bags, which keeps these gases in, and then we put them in our closets. YUCK!

Hint: *If you must dry clean your clothes, please do this: Take your clothing out of the plastic and hang it outside for a few hours before you bring these clothes into your closet. Remember to recycle the plastic you brought them home in.*

Other harmful dry cleaning methods involve hydrocarbon cleaning and a process using D5 cleaning. D5 is a silicone-based Dow chemical that goes by the name of Green Earth. They say it is completely safe for humans and the environment... so, maybe it only causes rats to grow tumors in their uterus. Dow chemical actually admitted that it does but says that it is "not relevant" to humans.[64]

A great resource for finding alternative, non-toxic dry cleaning methods near you is to visit www.nodryclean.com. Put in your zip code and see if there are any facilities close by; it is worth traveling the few extra miles though if not. When we invest in clothing made ethically and with natural fibers, we must think about our cleaning methods.

We have talked about ways to take care of clothing more consciously but where else could these toxins be lurking?

Have you ever sat down and thought about this? When you walk into a home after it has been cleaned, we are taught that is a "clean" smell. However, it is actually a very toxic smell from the chemicals in the toilet bowl cleaner, counter cleaner, window cleaner, carpet freshener (okay, that's kind of funny— freshen your carpet with chemicals), wood polisher, shower

---

64   https://chemicalwatch.com/30213/d5-causes-cancer-in-rats-but-not-relevant-to-humans

cleaner... I could go on and on. The idea is to lessen the load on our bodies. You live in your home and are being affected by these chemicals every single day.

If you want a clean stove, try this little tip. Take baking soda and water and make it into a paste. Put it on your cooktop and let it sit there for a few minutes. Cut a lemon in half and use it like a scrubber and move the baking soda around to remove the dirt. Wipe the mixture off with a warm cloth. Your cooktop will sparkle like new. The only smell left behind will be that of lemon juice! Now that smells clean!

How about your windows? Mix together Isopropyl alcohol, water, and vinegar. Wipe it on and watch your windows sparkle. Then just throw the rag in the washer and use it again. No wasteful paper towels needed.

When it comes to cleaning your clothes and your home, you need to simplify the process. This will not only cut down on chemicals being used in our homes, but it will also reduce all the packaging. This too ends up as waste in landfills. Let's commit to cutting down the load we are piling on Mother Nature!

Chapter 9

Brands We Love — Sustainable Shopping guide

This chapter is all about brands we love that are doing good things for the planet, humanity, and our future. NO SWEATSHOPS OR SLAVE LABOR HERE! Everyone is working hard to create change.

"Art changes people. People change the world"
— John Butler

WE BELIEVE FASHION IS ART.

Disclaimer: No individuals paid or were paid to have their brands included in this book. These are companies I have researched or been a customer of, and I cultivated this list to guide you on your path to sustainable shopping. No one company is doing everything perfectly, but all are moving in the right direction toward developing a more ethical business model that takes into consideration fair labor, environmental impact, and the toll on human and animal life today and in the future, as equally valued components of the supply chain. These companies strive to achieve sustainability in their fabrics, designs, finishes, dyes, work culture, and so much more.

I hope you find companies here you can get behind. I have represented men's, women's, and children's clothing in this list—everything from ready-to-wear to outerwear to intimates to active wear, as well as products for your skin and your home. Sustainability is the common thread. Read the information provided, but please visit their websites and educate yourself further. Remember, you hold the power to create the change!

"No one is doing everything, but everyone is doing something." — Tracey Martin

---

Ready-to-Wear

WOMEN'S APPAREL

1. Eileen Fisher

www.eileenfisher.com

Headquarters: New York, NY

Manufacturing Location: U.S.A. and China

Description: Elegant women's wear made from natural and organic fabrics in some collections. Eileen is leading an initiative calling for all businesses to be human rights conscious and sustainable by 2020.

Offerings: Women's apparel

Mission: "We are working to support the environment, human rights, and initiatives for women and girls."

2. *Kaizen Capsule*

www.shopkaizen.com

Headquarters: Scottsdale, AZ

Manufacturing Location: Tempe, AZ and Los Angeles, CA

Offerings: Women's ready-to-wear classic apparel with an elegant Bohemian twist.

Mission: "To present to the world that sustainable fashion can be stylish with classic silhouettes and mindful manufacturing. All our workers are paid fair wages and work in comfortable conditions with ethical practices. Our fabrics are GOTS-certified, natural fibers. Our dyes are GOTS, plant-based dyes. We use coconut buttons when needed, and all components are locally sourced, made in the USA."

3. Amour Vert

www.amourvert.com

Headquarters: San Francisco, CA

Manufacturing Location: U.S.A.

Description: Started by a husband and wife team in San Francisco, this company uses certified organic cotton in some of their designs and collaborations. They carpool their fabric deliveries with other local businesses to reduce their carbon footprint. Sustainable fashion made in the USA!

Offerings: Women's apparel

Mission: "We were founded on the belief that great fashion and social responsibility can coexist. Our name means 'green love' in French. We believe that together we can make the world a greener and more beautiful place, one garment at a time.

4. Zady

www.zady.com

Headquarters: New York, NY

Description: A feast for the eyes, Zady is committed to creating a lifestyle destination for conscious consumers. Sustainable, conscious, and ethically produced, this marketplace carries brands that are manufactured in the U.S.A. and all over the world.

Offerings: Women's apparel

Mission: "Fashion has a systemic issue. We are building a company that proves there is a better way...making clothes the way they should be."

5. ASOS

www.asos.com

Headquarters: Camden/London, England

Manufacturing Location: China and the U.K.

Description: Visit the green room for their ethically conscious brand committed to creating sustainable fashion to safeguard the future.

Offerings: Women's apparel

Mission: "Implementation of 4 pillars of philosophy:

    –Improved traceability of raw materials

    –Lower environmental impact

    –Craftsmanship

    –Engaging customers on sustainability practices."

6. Awave Awake

www.awaveawake.com

Headquarters: New York, NY

Manufacturing Location: U.S.A.

Description: Beautiful, naturally dyed, eco-friendly dresses and layering pieces for women. Reminds us of the 1960s and 1970s carefree style of flowing dresses.

Offerings: Women's apparel

Mission: "Striving to be a marriage of functionality and beauty. A conscious footprint and considerate of the world."

7. Study–NY

www.study-ny.com

Headquarters: New York, NY

Manufacturing Location: New York, NY

Offerings: Contemporary, sustainable women's wear

Mission: "We focus on every step of a product's journey. From field to cutting table, every part of the garment process is carefully examined and controlled to be socially and environmentally conscious."

8. Stella McCartney

www.stellamccartney.com

Headquarters: London, England

Manufacturing location: Worldwide

Offerings: Women's ready to wear, shoes, accessories, lingerie, eyewear, kids, and fragrance.

Mission: Stella launched her line in 2001. She is a lifelong vegetarian and activist. Therefore, she uses no leather or fur in her designs. Her commitment to sustainability is evident throughout her collections and is part of her brand's ethos to being responsible, honest, and modern.

9. The Reformation

www.thereformation.com

Headquarters: Los Angeles, CA

Manufacturing Location: Los Angeles, CA

Offerings: Women's apparel

Mission: "To lead and inspire a sustainable way to be fashionable using sustainable and vintage fabrics sourced in the USA and abroad. Making killer clothes that don't kill the environment."

10. Satva

www.satvaliving.com

Headquarters: New York

Manufacturing Location: U.S.A.

Offerings: A beautiful line of women's active wear and lounge wear

Mission: "We stand for 'seed to garment' production. We understand and celebrate cotton made from eco-friendly, non-GMO, bio ingredients. 100% organic cotton-made clothing."

11. Kordal Knitwear
www.kordalknitwear.com
Headquarters: Brooklyn, NY
Manufacturing Location: New York, NY
Offerings: Women's knits, sweaters, cardigans, and dresses
Mission: "To create garments in an ethical manner by paying our workers a fair wage and designing garments that are not trend-focused using natural fibers."

12. Wear Animal Behavior
www.wearanimalbeahavior.com
Headquarters: Los Angeles, CA
Manufacturing Location: Los Angeles, CA
Offerings: Women's ready-to-wear apparel
Mission: "Locally produced, sustainable, and socially responsible. We utilize a well thought out design, development, and production cycle. By doing this, we can reduce waste that is created from excessive sampling and over producing. 5% of all sales go to panthers.org."

13. Edun
www.edun.com
Headquarters: New York, NY
Manufacturing Location: Africa

Offerings: Women's apparel

Mission: "In respect of its mission to source production and encourage trade in Africa, Edun mixes its modern designer vision with the richness and positivity of this fast growing continent. Edun is building long-term sustainability growth opportunities by supporting manufacturers and community-based initiatives, and by partnering with African artists and artisans. Founded by Ali Hewson and Bono in 2005."

14. Beaumont Organic

www.beaumontorganic.com

Headquarters: London, U.K.

Manufacturing Location: U.K.

Offerings: Women's ready-to-wear dresses, tops, knits, bottoms, and accessories

Mission: Organic, sustainable, and educational components reign supreme with this brand.

15. YSTR

www.ystrclothing.com

Headquarters: Los Angeles, CA

Manufacturing Location: Los Angeles, CA

Offerings: Women's ready-to-wear, outerwear, and accessories

Mission: "We were founded to provide a better alternative to modern fashion shopping. We create clothes using sustainable and cut-to-order technologies to combat the waste in the current fashion industry."

16. Warriors Divine

www.warriorsdivine.com

Headquarters: Bali

Manufacturing Location: Bali

Description: Unique, hand-painted angel wing kimonos.

Offerings: Silk apparel for women

Mission: "My resolve is to create exquisite, handcrafted pieces that exist and have a story behind each one. Feel assured that the beautiful skilled Balinese workers who make my clothing receive fair wages and work under healthy conditions."

17. Synergy Clothing

www.synergyclothing.com

Headquarters: Santa Cruz, CA

Manufacturing Location: Nepal

Offerings: Fashion-forward clothing and yoga apparel for women

Mission: "Always striving to be mindful and conscious in every facet of our business, we produce sustainable and organic Fair Trade clothing that lets you look and feel your best.

18. Raven and Lily

www.ravenandlily.com

Headquarters: Austin, TX

Manufacturing Location: Global

Offerings: Women's apparel, jewelry, and bags in minimalist designs

Mission: "We were created to alleviate poverty among women. We currently help employ 1,500 marginalized women at Fair Trade wages to give them access to safe jobs, sustainable income, health care, and education."

19. Santa Marguerite

www.santamarguerite.com
Headquarters: Los Angeles, CA
Manufacturing Location: Mexico
Description: Bringing traditional techniques and folk patterns into the 21st century. Each piece is hand-stitched by artisanal manufacturers in Mexico. One-of-a-kind garments for one-of-a-kind style.
Offerings: Women's dresses, tops and tunics' bags, shoes, and children's apparel
Mission: "Our fashion line combines heritage and beautiful contemporary silhouettes while honoring tradition."

20. Mata Traders

www.matatraders.com
Headquarters: Chicago, IL
Manufacturing Location: India and Nepal
Offerings: Women's dresses, skirts and tops, jewelry and scarves; home décor
Mission: "We are a design-driven, ethical fashion company merging uncommon, vibrant style with our focus on changing global poverty."

21. Shaina Mote

www.shainamote.com

Headquarters: Los Angeles, CA

Manufacturing Location: Los Angeles, CA

Description: From the inception of a new design to the final product, all Shaina Mote pieces are designed, developed, and made in Los Angeles.

Offerings: Women's ready-to-wear

Mission: Dedication to fair, American-made production stands at the forefront of what they do and how they do it. From the beginning, they have been supporting the local economy and nurturing the trades and skills found within domestic garment manufacturing, using natural fibers for each collection.

22. Jesse Kamm

www.jessekamm.com

Headquarters: Los Angeles, CA

Manufacturing Location: Los Angeles, CA

Description: The kind of effortless, yet spot-on wardrobe you fantasize about wearing to a candlelit garden party in your dream life in sunny Southern California when you're actually in the middle of a harsh NYC winter. A collection of pared-down, but thoughtful pieces designed for impact and long-term wearability.

Offerings: Women's ready-to-wear

Mission: "To make strong clothing for strong women. Shapes that are minimal, clean and handsome, constructed to last.

Purchasing dead stock when possible to remain sustainable in manufacturing."

23. Alas the Label

www.alasthelabel.com
Headquarters: Australia
Manufacturing Location: India
Offerings: Women's sleepwear, ready-to-wear, and active wear
Mission: "Our philosophy is to shine a light on our manufacturing practices, following each piece from organically grown seed to the cloth that's made into garments under fair practices in India."

24. Our Hands for Hope

https://www.ourhandsforhope.com/
Headquarters: Napa, CA
Manufacturing Location: Trujillo, Peru (Also working in Southeast Asia and India with trafficking rescue homes.)
Offerings: Women's accessories, sweaters, tunics, ponchos, hats, gloves, scarves, handbags, and jewelry
Mission: "We believe in training, mentoring and empowering women in at-risk communities to create opportunities for economic sustainability."

25. Wear Thought

www.wearthought.com
Headquarters: UK

Manufacturing Location: China

Offerings: Organic cotton, bamboo, and hemp collections for women's apparel and swimwear

Mission: "We design and make beautiful, timeless fashion, while also caring for the environment. We believe in forging relationships with our factories and workers to ensure fair wages and working conditions. A thoughtful way of doing business."

26. NAJA

www.naja.co

Headquarters: San Francisco, CA

Manufacturing Location: Medellín, Colombia

Offerings: Artisan-made premium lingerie: underwear, bras, and panties

Mission: "We are serious about empowering women. We train single mothers in Colombia to sew handmade pieces. We have a deep desire to make the world a better place. We are the natural alternative to Victoria's Secret. We are going for the soul, not sex. Some items are even made from recycled plastic bottles."

27. All the Wild Roses

www.allthewildroses.com

Headquarters: NSW, Australia

Manufacturing Location: NSW, Australia

Offerings: Ultra-feminine dresses, tops, separates, jumpsuits, and accessories

Mission: "Bohemian fashion for the dreamers and change makers. We believe fashion is made for change. Ethical and philanthropic endeavors are important to us." Socially-conscious label.

28. LA Relaxed

www.larelaxed.com
Headquarters: Los Angeles, CA
Manufacturing Location: Los Angeles, CA
Offerings: Women's basic tees, dresses, skirts, and pants created from organic cotton, modal, and tencel fabrics
Mission: "Where it is made, who is making it and what it is made of is at the heart of LA Relaxed. We believe it's time for the eco-friendly fashion movement to expand and move forward."

29. Alexandria Main

www.alexandriamain.com
Headquarters: Queensland, Australia
Manufacturing Location: Cambodia
Offerings: Beach cover-ups, beach bags, robes, and skirts
Mission: "We believe fashion should be beautiful from the inside out. Our clothing is ethically made in Cambodia by studios that were established to empower their seamstresses. Cutting is done by hand and sewing is by hand because we want to teach skills."

30. Ankura

www.ankurabrand.com

Headquarters: Peru

Manufacturing Location: Peru

Description: Feminine, flattering pieces for today's woman that make a positive change. Their garments are a mix of the classic sophistication of natural fibers such as baby Alpaca, Pima cotton, organic cotton, and silk with trendy designs and a concern for society. They also offer accessories such as bracelets and keyrings, created by local artisans.

Mission: "We are a Peruvian brand that embraces the culture of fashion sustainability. Our main purpose is to bring positive change and progress through the creation of a new and improved fashion industry that promotes responsible brands, goods, and education for the future. Our supply chain is sourced locally. We partner with small local workshops and artisan communities. We investigate our environmental impact. We make responsible choices."

31. Stormie Dreams

www.stormiedreams.com

Headquarters: Los Angeles, CA

Manufacturing Location: Los Angeles, CA

Offerings: Women's ready-to-wear, dresses, skirts, shirts, jumpsuits, and intimates

Mission: "We make it our personal mission to create something bigger than just a business – we seek to inspire change in the fashion industry. As we continue to proudly produce USA-made fashion and uphold our sustainable practices, we will always strive to improve and empower the lives of others along the way. Our fabrics are 'rescued' from otherwise ending up in the landfill. Sustainability and philanthropy."

32. Only Hearts

www.onlyhearts.com
Headquarters: New York, NY
Manufacturing Location: New York, NY
Offerings: Organic cotton lingerie, dresses, robes, tops and bottoms
Mission: "Since 1978, we've been creating lingerie and clothing made for the shameless romantic to be worn anytime and anywhere!"

33. Have Love Must Travel

www.havelovemusttravel.com
Headquarters: New York, NY
Manufacturing Location: New Delhi, India
Offerings: Women's block printed dresses and tops
Mission: "We ethically produce sophisticated Boho clothing using hand-carved block prints by artisans in India. The block printing method is an ancient craft passed down through generations in the East."

34. Vyayama

www.vyayama.com
Headquarters: New York, NY

Manufacturing Location: Portugal

Offerings: Yoga wear and casual wear made with an innovative tencel fabric that is sustainably sourced from bamboo farms. An ethical ath-leisure brand.

Mission: "An ethical ath-leisure brand we founded with the intention of providing a natural alternative to synthetic yoga wear, with the belief that the products we use should be held to the same standards we hold ourselves to. We believe that mindfulness should inspire quality, beauty, and joy. Vyayama is a 3,000-year-old Sanskrit word meaning 'to move'."

35. Pitusa

www.pitusa.co

Headquarters: Peru

Manufacturing Location: Peru

Offerings: High-quality, comfortable and affordable beachwear for women: cover-ups, dresses, and beachwear produced from the finest Peruvian cottons, using a vibrant color palette and signature Inca trims.

Mission: "We focus on continuing to create clothing that empowers women, while offering a lighthearted aesthetic, transitioning easily from the beach to the street."

36. Kowtow

www.kowtowclothing.com

Headquarters: New Zealand

Manufacturing Location: Kolkata, India

Offerings: Everyday basic and collection pieces for women made from certified ethical organic cotton.

Mission: "We are committed to do something about the current state of the fashion industry. Certified organic, Fair Trade clothing that is ethically and sustainably made from seed to garment."

37. Style Saint

www.stylesaint.com

Headquarters: Los Angeles, CA

Manufacturing Location: Los Angeles, CA

Offerings: Women's ready-to-wear; everyday lace, luxe essentials; silk staples, dresses, tops, bottoms, and lingerie

Mission: "We are driven by our belief that with the customer's help we can change the world for the better. Join us and be the change that has the power to revolutionize an industry."

38. Vetta Capsule

www.vettacapsule.com

Headquarters: New York, NY

Manufacturing Location: New York, NY

Offerings: Women's ready-to-wear; five pieces that can create 30 different outfits

Mission: "We are committed to environmentally-friendly fabrics and responsible factories. Our clothing is made in a family-run factory in New York. We believe style can be sustainable."

39. Behno

www.behno.com

Headquarters: New York, NY

Manufacturing Location: Gujarat, India

Offerings: High-quality, luxurious and tailored women's designs: dresses, tops, bottoms, and outerwear

Mission: "We believe that luxury design can be done with ethical thinking. We believe garment workers are not a commodity and the fashion industry does not need to be based on the exploitation of labor."

40. Nicole Bridger

www.nicolebridger.com

Headquarters: Vancouver, B.C.

Manufacturing Location: Mount Pleasant, Vancouver, B.C.

Offerings: Women's dresses, tops, bottoms, jackets, cardigans, and maternity wear

Mission: "We are creating a path to a more caring and empowering existence. We create lifestyle products and conversations that support ethical and inspired living."

41. Tonle'

www.tonle.com

Headquarters: Cambodia

Manufacturing Location: Cambodia

Offerings: Women's dresses, tops, bottoms, and accessories

Mission: "At Tonle' we see fashion differently—from the way it's made to the way it's worn. We see it as encouraging the unique in everyone who touches our clothing, from maker to wearer."

42. LVR Fashion

www.lvrfashion.com

Headquarters: Los Angeles, CA

Manufacturing Location: Los Angeles, CA

Offerings: Earth-friendly active wear ethically made in the USA with a portion of revenue benefiting wildlife.

Mission: "We believe in apparel that gives back. We partner with a wildlife rescue center in Guatemala called ARCAS. Our donations help in the rescue, rehabilitation, and release of wild animals."

43. Sak Saum

www.saksaum.com

Headquarters: Cambodia

Manufacturing Location: Phnom Penh & Saang District, Cambodia

Offerings: Apparel, bags, scarves, jewelry, and accessories

Mission: "Our goal has been to create a nurturing, empow-ering, restorative program that facilitates vocational training in sewing, excellent products, and community development. This is how the battle against human trafficking will be won: one person, one family, one community at a time."

44. Seam Siren

www.seamsiren.com

Headquarters location: Maui, Hawaii

Manufacturing Location: Los Angeles, CA

Offerings: Medicinal clothing and accessories. Beautiful bags, wraps and accessories.

Mission: Bringing the healing wisdom of plants to the fashion industry through the ancient modality of medicinal clothing with the highest standard of transparency, integrity and purity. "Wear your medicine." is our tagline.

45. BYT brand

www.bytlife.com

Headquarters location: Hong Kong

Manufacturing Location: China, Thailand and New York

Offerings: Inaugural collection of up-cycled tailored jackets. Ranging from $250 USD - $350 USD. So much more coming soon!

Mission: We are on a passionate mission to create high quality clothes that you will love to live in. We take painstaking steps at the product level to bring you the best possible garment. Simply saying we create beautiful, up-cycled pieces that are timeless with a twist, it is affordable luxury.

46. Study.34

www.study34.co.uk

Headquarters: Newcastle, UK

Manufacturing Location: London

Offerings: Modern sustainable luxury for women

Mission: Champion those who empower, and do not exploit. Celebrate diversity and individuality.

MEN'S APPAREL

1. Saltura

www.saltura.co

Headquarters: Santa Barbara, CA

Manufacturing Location: Los Angeles, CA

Offerings: Men's tees, swim trunks, hats, and glasses inspired by life on the California coast

Mission: "We had a realization that nearly everything we wore was responsible for harming the environment and the ocean. We created Saltura, a line of elevated basics and beach essentials that feature sustainable fabrics. Modern, minimal design, and local manufacturing."

2. Apolis (Means "Global Citizen")

www.apolisglobal.com

Headquarters: SoHo, NY

Manufacturing Location: Bangladesh, Uganda, Peru, India, Ethiopia, Israel, and Honduras

Offerings: Artisan made men's jackets, shirts, sweaters, pants, denim, swimwear, and accessories

Mission: "We founded Apolis believing that business can create social change. We created a business model that bridges commerce and economic development."

3. Outerknown

www.outerknown.com

Headquarters: Southern California

Manufacturing Location: Peru, China, Mexico, Sri Lanka, and California

Offerings: Men's apparel, trunks, button-down shirts, board shorts, tees, and outerwear

Mission: "Smash the formula and lift the lid on the traditional supply chain to prove you can produce great looking menswear in a sustainable way. We were born on questioning and challenging the norms of clothing manufacturing." Created by world-renowned surfer, Kelly Slater.

MEN, WOMEN'S, AND CHILDREN'S

1. Industry of All Nations
www.industryofallnations.com

Headquarters: Los Angeles, CA

Description: Design and development office founded with a commitment to rethink methods of production for consumer goods. This site is great for learning about how to shop in a more ethical and sustainable way.

Offerings: Men's and women's apparel and footwear

Mission: "We are excited about how things get done. To provide opportunities to those manufacturing ethically and sustainably."

2. Triarchy
www.triarchy.com

Headquarters: Los Angeles, CA

Manufacturing Location: Los Angeles, CA and Mexico City,

Offerings: Denim jeans and jackets

Mission: "To conserve our planet's most important resource by reducing the massive water consumption of our planet's most beloved piece of clothing, jeans!"

3. Deadwood

www.deadwood.se

Headquarters: Sweden

Manufacturing Location: Sweden

Offerings: Men's and women's apparel and outerwear

Mission: "Celebrating ageless rebellion. Using recycled leather and cotton to create biker chic style. A cool edge and vintage feel."

4. Thinking MU

www.thinkingmu.com

Headquarters: Barcelona, Spain

Manufacturing Location: India and Peru

Offerings: Men's and women's apparel

Mission: "We believe that life is for living intensely, without limits. We produce 100% organic cotton products all designed in Barcelona."

5. NAU

www.nau.com

Headquarters: Portland, OR and Santa Rosa, CA

Manufacturing Location: U.S.A, Canada, China, and Thailand

Description: Fabrics are from China, Japan, Korea, and New Zealand. (Manufacturing in China is a must for this brand to keep its carbon footprint down because most of the fabrics are from the same region.)

Offerings: Men's and women's apparel

Mission: "Designing sustainable performance apparel that protects you in every environment. Sustainability comes standard."

6. Threads of Peru

www.threadsofperu.com

Headquarters: Cuzco, Peru

Manufacturing Location: Andes Mountains, Peru

Offerings: Men's and women's artisan ponchos, hats, gloves, scarves, and home décor

Mission: "We are a non-profit social enterprise that connects the world to handmade treasures of the Andes, helping to strengthen ancient craft techniques and empower artisans."

7. Threads 4 Thought

www.threads4thought.com

Headquarters: New York, NY

Manufacturing Location: China, Kenya, and India

Offerings: Men's and women's apparel and active wear

Mission: "We design and produce ethical, sustainable fashion that helps improve the planet we all share. We work with factory partners that are committed to ethical manufacturing and travel the world to build relationships with the owners, management, and workers who share our values."

8. Indigenous Designs

www.indigenous.com

Headquarters: Sebastopol, CA

Manufacturing Location: Global partners world-wide

Offerings: Men's and women's apparel, dresses, tops, pants, sweaters, ponchos, outwear, and accessories

Mission: "Organic and Fair Trade ethical fashion. Commitments are steadfast, even as fashion trends come and go. Supporting and preening Fair Trade wages and artisan cooperation."

9. Human Revolution Clothing

www.humanrevolutionclothing.com

Headquarters: Hawaii

Manufacturing Location: India

Offerings: Men's and women's ready-to-wear made from organic cotton and produced with Fair Trade wages

Mission: "HRC is a social, economic, environmental and LOVE-centered clothing company that is passionate about and dedicated to changing the way clothing is made—seed to shirt."

10. Faherty

www.faherty.com

Headquarters: New York, NY

Manufacturing Location: Peru, India, China, and U.S.A.

Offerings: Swimwear made primarily from recycled plastic bottles. Men's swimwear is a blend of recycled polyester and cotton. Women's is a blend of recycled polyester and Lycra for fit. Knits are dyed with a natural indigo dye. Organic cotton is used for woven shirts.

Mission: "Our lifelong dream is to create clothing for life's greatest moments—the ones spent by water, around a bonfire, catching waves or watching the sunrise. We're proud to custom design our fabrics, including our sustainable swimwear and develop relationships with our manufacturers to craft the highest quality goods."

11. Untouched World New Zealand

Headquarters: South Island, New Zealand

Manufacturing Location: South Island, New Zealand

Description: A full lifestyle brand and the first fashion company to be recognized by the UN for sustainability.

Offerings: Women's, men's, and children's clothing and home decor.

Mission: "Our full commitment is to action-based missions of the Clinton Global Initiative. We commit to raising the health and well-being of current and future generations by teaching comprehensive awareness programs for society to use as a basic template for building a better world."

12. Everlane

www.everlane.com

Headquarters: San Francisco, CA

Manufacturing Location: San Francisco, CA

Offerings: Men's and women's modern luxury wardrobe basics

Mission: "Know your factories, know the costs, and always ask questions. We choose to sell solely online, so we can have a more manageable price point."

13. Pendelton

www.pendelton.com

Headquarters: Portland, OR

Manufacturing Location: U.S.A.

Description: A family-run business since 1863. They stuck it out and remained dedicated to producing their products locally and responsibly, using 100-year-old mills in the Northwest.

Offerings: Men's and women's ready-to-wear, outerwear, bags, and accessories; home decor and accents

Mission: Completely committed to using sustainable wool and recycling materials and working on conserving water in their production processes.

14. Imogene and Willie

www.imogeneandwillie.com

Headquarters: Nashville, TN

Manufacturing Location: Los Angeles, CA

Offerings: Custom-made men's and women's denim, vintage tees and odds and ends

Mission: "To create something that we couldn't find: a perfectly fitting pair of jeans. Or, perhaps more precisely, to make perfect jeans for our imperfect bodies.

15. People Tree

www.peopletree.co.uk

Headquarters: London, UK

Manufacturing Location: Global

Offerings: Men's and women's clothing that makes you feel good and look good at the same time

Mission: "We aim to be 100% Fair Trade throughout our supply chain. People Tree purchases Fair Trade products from marginalized producer groups in developing countries. To purchase, to protect, to supply, to provide, and to set an example."

16. Fibre Athletics

www.fibreathletics.com

Headquarters: Portland, OR

Manufacturing Location: U.S.A.

Offerings: Men's and women's athletic wear and leisurewear

Mission: "We believe in ethical performance wear that is functional, sleek, and durable. No guilt; no toxins; no waste; no sweat; no junk; no overkill; and no hiding."

17. Mighty Good Undies

www.mightgoodundies.com.au

Headquarters: Australia

Manufacturing Location: India

Offerings: Men's and women's underwear and tees

Mission: "Everybody should have affordable, quality cotton underwear sourced from the most ethical and sustainable supply chain we can find. We think they should come with a carbon offset too.

18. Slum Love

www.slumlove.com

Headquarters: Los Angeles, CA

Manufacturing Location: Nairobi, Kenya

Offerings: Hand-knitted men's and women's sweaters, cardigans, and scarves

Mission: "We believe fashion can be a force for good. From our products to our packaging, we use only 100% natural organic and recycled materials. We give back to a non-profit that provides high school scholarships to children living in one of the world's largest slums."

19. Groceries Apparel

www.groceriesapparel.com

Headquarters: Los Angeles, CA

Manufacturing Location: Downtown Los Angeles, CA

Offerings: Men's and women's basics created out of natural fibers such as eucalyptus, recycled plastic, and organic cotton

Mission: "To create everyday basics with ethical and sustainable practices."

20. good hYOUman

www.goodhyouman.com

Headquarters & Manufacturing: Los Angeles, CA

Offerings: Men's and women's tees and accessories

Mission: "Our goal is to create and deliver YOU unbelievable, comfortable clothing and unique accessories that make YOU feel GOOD. Live Limitless."

21. Lovjoi

www.lovjoi.com

Headquarters: Germany

Manufacturing Location: Southern Germany

Offerings: Organic men's and women's apparel made from beautiful fabrics with comfortable silhouettes and lasting styles

Mission: "We believe in a small carbon footprint. The heart of our team is what moves this brand forward."

22. Kings of Indigo

www.kingsofindigo.com

Headquarters: The Netherlands

Manufacturing: Tunisia, India, and Italy

Offerings: Men's and women's denim jeans and shirts; knit-wear, t-shirts, and small leather goods

Mission: "Our goal and mission is to make quality products where the quality goes beyond itself. Quality of work environment is just as important. KOI cares about the people who make these great garments. We are a member of the Fair Wear Foundation, whose mission is to improve labor standards in the clothing industry."

23. Krochet Kids Intl.

www.krochetkids.com

Headquarters: Costa Mesa, CA

Manufacturing Location: Uganda and Peru

Offerings: Men's, women's, and children's apparel; headwear, bags, and accessories—every piece is signed by the person who created it

Mission: "Through a unique model, we are empowering the women of Northern Uganda and Peru with the assets, skills, and knowledge to lift themselves and their families out of poverty. Jobs, education, and mentorship."

24. Patagonia

www.patagonia.com

Headquarters: Ventura, CA

Manufacturing Location: 75 factories around the world, including Fair Trade Certified factories in the U.S.A.

Offerings: Men's, women's, children's, and baby apparel and outwear; outdoor gear, bags, and backpacks

Mission: "Build the best product, cause no unnecessary harm, and use business to inspire and implement solutions to the environmental crisis."

25. Pact Organic

www.wearpact.com

Headquarters: Boulder, CO

Manufacturing Location: India

Description: Lots of fun patterns on products made from organic cotton. It is better for the planet, farmers, factory workers, and YOU, the customer!

Offerings: Super-soft men's, women's, and baby basics

Mission: "Change you can wear! Using organic cotton and low-impact dyes for all products. We believe the right way to make clothes is to care for the rights of the people who make them. We work with GOTS to certify all of our supply chain."

26. NOCTU

www.noctu.co.uk

Headquarters: Bath, UK

Manufacturing Location: Oslo, Norway

Offerings: Organic cotton sleepwear and loungewear for men, women, and children

Mission: "Our desire is to create ethically-made, beautiful, minimal night and loungewear with the lowest impact on the planet and people."

27. Armor Lux

wwww.amorlux.com

Headquarters: Quimper, France

Manufacturing Location: Quimper, France

Offerings: Men's, women's, and children's ready-to-wear fashions and underwear; collections are inspired by the French maritime tradition and values conveyed by the sea.

Mission: "Founded in 1938, our three core values are quality, innovation, and ethics. We are resolutely committed to sustainable development. We respect human rights, the health of our customers, and protection of the environment."

28. Boody

www.boody.com.au

Headquarters: San Diego, CA

Manufacturing Location: Sydney, Australia

Offerings: Organic bamboo eco-wear for men, women, and babies: tops, underwear, leggings, and socks

Mission: "We are on a mission to create clothes that are soft, sensible, and good for the world. Live and enjoy. Our bamboo is plantation-grown and requires much less water than cotton-based fabrics."

29. Recover Brands

www.recoverbrands.com
Headquarters: Charlotte, NC
Manufacturing Location: Charlotte, NC, and Haiti
Offerings: Men's, women's, and youth tees and hoodies
Mission: "We work to make the most environmentally friendly products possible. We also strive to make the most socially responsible products possible. All Recover garments begin at the source: recycled plastic bottles and recycled cotton."

30. Spiritex

www.spiritex.net
Headquarters: Asheville, NC
Manufacturing Location: Asheville, NC
Offerings: Men's, women's, and children's apparel
Mission: "Grown and sewn in the U.S.A. In a globalized world, full of the same but different, Spiritex is inspired to be the change we wanted to see. Our concern for sustainable and ethically minded manufacturing and equality within the global community was the catalyst that sparked the passion behind Spiritex fashion."

31. California Cloth Foundry

www.clothfoundry.com

Headquarters: San Francisco, CA.

Manufacturing location: Multiple sites from the Southeast USA to California

Offerings: CCF is 100% all natural luxury for "A Healthy Wardrobe." We make stylish, unique apparel and linens for the whole family to live in. We supply textiles to slow fashion labels and eco-conscious designers.

Mission: CCF uses a collaborative-development approach, working directly with farms, ranches, and the entire textile/apparel supply chain to provide 100% farm-to-fashion non-toxic fabrications and fashion while ensuring fair wages throughout the supply chain.

32. Ramblers Way

www.ramblersway.com

Headquarters: Kennebunk, Maine

Manufacturing Location: North Carolina and Massachusetts

Offerings: Ramblers way uses Rambouillet merino wool and pima cottons. Both sustainable natural fibers. Styles include tops, bottoms, dress, skirts and seasonal essentials for both men and women. Clothing for a good life. Truly premium apparel crafted to work for your wardrobe and your sustainable lifestyle.

Mission: To work with nature to make responsibly sources, skillfully crafted, American made sustainable clothing.

DENIM

1. Tellason

www.tellason.com

Manufacturing Location: San Francisco, CA

Materials: Cone denim in Greensboro, NC and all U.S.A. components, thread, label, rivets, and zippers

Description: Tellason sells raw denim, which means it has not been wet processed or manipulated in any way. That is where the fun comes in! The wearer creates the character in each pair of jeans. These jeans are built to last!

2. Hiut Denim

www.hiutdenim.co.uk

Manufacturing location: Cardigan, UK

Materials: Selvedge denim

Description: At Hiut, they claim "to do one thing and do one thing well," which is make amazing denim. They have a Breakers Club, a group of local people who break in all denim before it is sold. The goal was to get people in their town back to work and give them jobs. The company also has an option to join their No Wash Club, where you don't wash your jeans for six months after purchasing them. Freezing is allowed and airing them out on the clothes line is allowed. After six months, you will have the most incredible pair of jeans you have ever owned! Trust me!

3. Left Field NYC

www.leftfieldnyc.com

Manufacturing Location: New York, NY

Materials: Raw selvedge denim, chino twill, cotton, and hemp

Description: Left Field NYC was started back in 1998 when American-made clothing was unheard of. They aim to create clothing that "our grandfathers would be proud of."

4. Free Note Cloth

www.freenotecloth.com

Manufacturing Location: San Juan Capistrano, CA

Materials: This company claims to only source the highest quality denim and components from the Cone mills in the U.S. and the Yoshiwa mills in Japan.

Description: They create classic American menswear and honor tradition by manufacturing their collection exclusively in the United States.

5. Nudie Jeans

www.nudiejeans.com

Headquarters: Gothenburg, Sweden

Manufacturing Location: India and Europe

Offerings: Unisex organic denim products. Mens jeans and children's wear.

Mission: This company is a shining example of circular sustainable practices. They only use organic cotton. They are committed to providing reports for a transparent supply chain. They are committed to social responsibility through fair wages to all their workers. They purchase their Fair-trade cotton from Chetna Organics, an Indian non-government organization. Their jeans can be repaired, resold as second hand or even donated to Nudie jeans recycling program where they were purchased.

6. Monkee Genes

www.monkeegenes.com

Headquarters: United Kingdom

Manufacturing Location: Indonesia, Turkey and England

Offerings: Mens and women's organic denim. Numerous cuts and fits available. Also, offering organic tees.

Mission: We make ethical jeans because we care. We were created to to bring out true rhythm from your natural sensitivity. Monkey Genes was born in 2006 out of the frustration of the denim market in the UK. We will continue to work towards a new and prosperous future.

7. Kuyichi

www.kuyichi.com

Headquarters Location: Amsterdam, Netherlands

Manufacturing Location: Tunisia, Turkey and Greece

Offerings: Organic denim for men and women. They also offer a full line of organic cotton shirts, sweaters and knitwear.

Mission: We believe in taking the environmental, and social responsibility to action. This includes more than making just good products at the right price. Our love is the concept of bringing slow fashion to the market. We know that a beautiful pair of jeans keeps its value. That is why we have let go of the notion of "seasonal collections".

Footwear

WOMEN'S SHOES

Mink Shoes

www.minkshoes.com

Headquarters: Venice, California

Manufacturing Location: Italy

Offerings: Luxe vegan shoes hand made in Italy. Stilettos, sandals, and ballet flats. They will even do a custom pair for you.

Mission: To create vegan luxury shoes from sustainable products such as wood, cork, bamboo, non animal glue, vegetable resins, organic and recycled fabrics. Absolute luxury, cruelty-free.

MEN'S AND WOMEN'S SHOES

1. Nisolo

www.nisolo.com

Headquarters: Trujillo, Peru & Nashville, TN

Manufacturing Location: Peru, Mexico, and Kenya

Offerings: Men's and women's shoes

Mission: "Nisolo means 'not alone.' We view our social impact in two ways: game changing and life changing. Artisan products empowering communities."

2. All Birds

www.allbirds.com

Headquarters: New Zealand

Manufacturing Location: New Zealand

Offerings: Men's and women's footwear created out of merino wool

Mission: "We have a vision to do things differently. We think less is more, which is why we don't include unnecessary logos or detailing. Instead, we designed the simplest, most comfortable shoe we could using premium materials, without the premium price. They minimize odor, regulate temperature and wick moisture."

3. Nae

www.nae-vegan.com

Headquarters: Portugal

Manufacturing Location: Portugal

Offerings: Stylish vegan shoes for men and women

Mission: "Nae was born under the assumption of no animal exploitation but also focused on the design, style, and quality that is already recognized in Portuguese shoes. We propose a fair and animal-friendly alternative against human exploitation with respect for the environment."

4. Poppy Barley

www.poppybarleycom

Headquarters: Canada

Manufacturing Location: Leon, Mexico

Offerings: Women's and men's shoes and boots

Mission: "We are not willing to sacrifice social responsibility for luxury. Our shoes are made in family-owned factories screened for ethical working conditions. We are still striving for more transparency in our supply chain and welcome our customers' input."

5. Veja

www.veja-store.com

Headquarters: France and Brazil

Manufacturing Location: France and Brazil

Offerings: Ecological sneakers, bags, and accessories for men, women, and kids; Fair Trade footwear and accessories

Mission: "We offer a different vision that combines Fair Trade and ecology and links together economy, social initiative, and the environment. A vision that proposes cultural change."

6. Movmt

www.thepeoplesmovement.com

Headquarters: Solano Beach, California

Manufacturing Location: Bali & California

Offerings: Men's and women's shoes and accessories. Low top and Hi tops available. We also offer small handbags and wallets.

Mission: The Peoples Movement was born from the desire to create shoes and accessories for friends that reflected our passion for clean design and a clean environment. We are driven to be the positive change we want to see in the world. We create eco-hip footwear that stand for reduction in single use plastic.

SOCKS & TIGHTS

2. Osom Brand

www.osombrand.com

Headquarters: Florida

Manufacturing Location: U.S.A.

Offerings: Sustainably made socks for men and women

Mission: "We are committed to being part of the change. We are not just a trend; we are a sustainable brand simply representing the future of the textile industry and how things should be done from this point forward. By making high-quality, upcycled clothing, we are closing the loop in the fashion industry."

3. Tibetan Socks

www.tibetansocks.com

Headquarters: Los Angeles, CA

Manufacturing Location: The Himalayas

Offerings: Super-cozy wool slipper socks for the entire family

Mission: "We are committed to maintaining a socially responsible organization with integrated values based on the Dharma (Buddha's teachings). Each pair of socks sold gives back to those in need by providing food, medicine, education materials, and other essentials throughout the Himalayan region. Thoughtful, social and ethical."

4. Swedish Stocking Company

www.swedishstockings.com

Headquarters: Stockholm, Sweden

Manufacturing Location: Sweden

Offerings: Women's tights and stockings

Mission: "We are proud to combine sustainability, quality, and great design and hope that you will feel the same pride. We are constantly looking for cleaner ways to produce, conserve or reuse water, decreasing emissions, reducing and recycling waste. From our highly efficient recycling procedures, we have reduced energy and water consumption by 87.6%. A large part of our production is solar-powered. Our factory is zero waste. All water used for dyeing is purified and treated."

Accessories

WOMEN'S

1. Alexandra K

www.alexandrak.co

Headquarters: Krakow, Poland

Manufacturing: Krakow, Poland

Offerings: Beautiful vegan handbags.

Mission: "Our mission is to create beautiful bags that are environmentally friendly and use no animal products."

2. La Bonte London

www.labante.co.uk

Headquarters: London

Manufacturing Location: London

Mission: Our bags and jewelry are not only covetable but also vegan, environmentally friendly, and ethically produced. We want to give consumers the experience of luxury, of the finest craftsmanship, and of a timeless aesthetic while respecting the world we live in.

Offerings: Women's handbags, small goods, and jewelry

Mission: For us "Fashion with Respect" implies that we consider all living beings and the planet. It's more than our mission or philosophy. It's the way we work, live, and breathe. We are leading a change in the luxury industry ensuring that our tomorrow will present us elegant products that are ethical and sustainable—products we can both enjoy and be proud of.

3. Flux Productions Accessories

www.fluxproductions.net

Headquarters: Brooklyn, NY

Manufacturing Location: Brooklyn, NY

Description: All items are made by hand in a craftsman studio located in Fort Greene.

Offerings: An array of vintage t-shirts, leather bags, and small accessories

Mission: "We are a small artisan studio. Our emphasis is on care and craft instead of mass production."

4. Meyelo

www.meyelo.com

Headquarters: Pennsylvania

Manufacturing Location: Kenya

Description: Artisan products made by over 80 women living in Kenya.

Offerings: Bags, jewelry, beads, scarves, and sandals

Mission: "Empowering artisans with sustainable income through their craft. Investing in small business in developing countries brings social and economic change."

5. A Peace Treaty

www.apeacetreaty.com

Headquarters: New York, NY

Manufacturing Location: Afghanistan, Bangladesh, Bolivia, Ecuador, India, and the USA

Offerings: Women's accessories, capes, caftans, scarves, hats, and jewelry

Mission: "Founded on the belief that things made by human hands, imbued with the story of the maker, are the most beautiful and luxurious in the world."

6. Ono Creations

www.onocreations.com

Headquarters: Switzerland

Manufacturing Location: Europe

Offerings: Elegantly and ethically handcrafted handbags. These vegan bags are also Peta approved. The main material is cork and a leather substitute made from tencel. Other materials used are organic bamboo, organic cotton and natural plant based pigments for dyeing.

Mission: We imagine a world in which fashion is crafted and enjoyed with passion. A world that preserves nature through the creation of beautiful products. Our philosophy is "cause no harm." We live it every day.

7. Beekeeper Backpacks

www.beekeeperparade.com

Headquarters: Melbourne, Australia

Manufacturing Location: Cambodia

Offerings: Backpacks, travel bags, and accessories. Made from vegan and sustainable materials.

Mission: We create products that inspire change. Our backpacks will tackle the world's massive textile waste issues head-on whilst funding the English program for a school in rural Cambodia, giving each child a rich future of quality education. We take our environmental responsibility very seriously!

8. Angela Roi

www.angelaroi.com

Headquarters: Bostons, Massachusetts

Manufacturing location: Seoul, Korea

Offerings: Handbags, small goods, and accessories

Mission: We are created on the foundation of kindness, values, and love. Our bags are produced from the highest quality of vegan leather. We believe that there is no need for fashion to be cruel. We aim to create a different kind of luxury.

9. Ruda Rings & Pendants

www.aneisruda.com.br

Headquarters: Belo Horizonte, Brazil

Manufacturing Location: Belo Horizonte, Brazil

Offerings: Artisan hand-crafted rings made from Brazilian hardwoods

Mission: "Everything is useful. Our wood is sourced from discarded, high-quality furniture, and salvage houses. The raw stones are from around the world. Each piece ships in a recycled coffee bag."

10. Akola Project

www.akolaproject.org
Headquarters: Dallas, TX
Manufacturing Location: Uganda
Offerings: Necklaces, earrings, and bracelets created with paper beads and semi-precious stones
Mission: "Our jewelry is designed to empower women in disadvantaged communities throughout the globe. AKOLA means 'she works' in Lusoga. We are a full-impact brand that trains and employs women in poverty.

11. The Starfish Project

www.thestarfishproject.com
Headquarters: Goshen, IN
Manufacturing Location: Asia
Offerings: Beautiful necklaces, earrings, and bracelets
Mission: "Restoring hope to exploited women. We believe everyone has worth. We built a shelter so women who have escaped sex trafficking have a place to go. Our jewelry provides jobs and income for them to help themselves, their families, and communities. Our core values are growth, authentic relationships, celebrating people, and excellence."

12. Emilime

www.shopemilime.com

Headquarters: Lima, Peru

Manufacturing Location: Peru

Offerings: Handmade accessories that feature materials from alpaca and highland sheep wool

Mission: "We are committed to sourcing the highest quality materials working with Peruvian makers and knitters." Emily, the founder, works with and believes in empowering the artisans and leaders in the community, so an investment is made in the relationships, education, and craft of the individuals within the community.

13. Tribe Alive

www.shoptribealive.com

Headquarters: Forth Worth, TX

Manufacturing Location: Honduras, Guatemala, India, and Haiti

Offerings: Women's accessories.

Mission: "Our mission is to build sustainable partnerships with marginalized groups in developing countries by connecting them to the global marketplace. We work to break the cycle of poverty by providing artisans with the tools, training, and support needed to reclaim their futures and thrive as independent business men and women."

14. OOD-ITALY

http://www.ood-italy.it

Headquarters: Rome, Italy

Manufacturing Location: Italy

Offerings: Beautiful accessories made from wood

Mission: "OOD is committed to a beauty that is also good. We believe that making an eco-compatible choice does not mean to sacrifice design. Sustainability is not just a word. We support reforestation projects throughout the world."

14. Threads of Evolution

www.threadsofevolution.com

Headquarters: Scottsdale, AZ

Manufacturing Location: Los Angeles, CA

Offerings: Womens handbags and accessories. We offer a wide range beautiful weekenders, hobos, messengers as well as small clutches and zippered pouches.

Mission: We believe in the craft of the artisan. We believe that true luxury takes time and is respected. We believe that our products should stand the test of time and only get better the more you use them. The body of our bag is the Chindi rug which is handmade in India. Our bags are then handcrafted in small production runs in L.A. artisan families. A story is sewn into each bag which talks about the evolution of all of us.

MEN'S AND WOMEN'S ACCESSORIES
1. The Base Project

www.thebaseproject.com

Headquarters: Waikiki, HI

Manufacturing Location: Africa

Offerings: Men's and women's hand-carved wrist cuffs made from silver, gold, and recycled, carved PVC

Mission: The Base Project is a socially motivated brand building a bridge between artisans in the developing world and the U.S. fashion market. Through fashion products, they create jobs and invest in community development projects.

2. The Giving Keys

www.thegivingkeys.com

Headquarters: Los Angeles, CA

Manufacturing Location: Los Angeles, CA

Offerings: Men's and women's necklaces and bracelets made from keys imprinted with positive messages

Mission: "We exist to employ those transitioning out of homeless shelters in Los Angeles to make key necklaces and other jewelry out of repurposed keys."

3. Matt and Nat

www.mattandnat.com

Headquarters: Montreal, Quebec

Manufacturing Location: China

Offerings: A collection of design-centric, eco-friendly, and vegan accessories including bags, wallets, and shoes

Mission: "Matt (short for material) and Nat (short for nature). We live a simple motto, 'Live beautifully,' meaning appreciation for humanity, creativity, and positivity found in all of us.

Home Goods

1. Under the Canopy

www.underthecanopy.com

Headquarters: New York, NY

Manufacturing Location: Virginia

Offerings: GOTS-certified organic home goods, bedding, towels, and basic apparel

Mission: "Conscience without compromise. Working hard to create a change within the industry."

2. Coyuchi

www.coyuchi.com

Headquarters: Northern California

Manufacturing Location: California

Offerings: Home goods made with natural fibers: bedding, towels, sheets, table linen; also, a small assortment of robes, pajamas, and outerwear for men, women, and children

Mission: "To be the source for organic cotton and natural home furnishings that respects our environment and enhances the lives of every one of our customers. People, planet, and process."

3. Seljak

www.seljak.com

Headquarters: Australia

Manufacturing Location: Tasmania

Offerings: Recycled merino wool blankets made from the off-cuts from the factory floor: merino wool, alpaca, mohair, and recycled polyester

Mission: "To close the loop. We are two sisters who imagine a world without waste. Once you have enjoyed your blanket and no longer want it, we will collect it free of charge through a carbon neutral courier. It will be shredded and re-spun to create another blanket."

4. The Oriole Mill

www.theoriolemill.com

Headquarters: Hendersonville, NC

Manufacturing Location: Hendersonville, NC

Offerings: Women's wraps; home goods, bedding, blankets, pillows, shams, and throws

Mission: "What we don't do is as important as what we do. We think it is most important to make products that last and to make them from natural fibers."

5. Elkie and Ark

www.elkieark.com

Headquarters: Australia

Manufacturing Location: Telangana, India

Offerings: We produce beautiful organic and sustainable classic bedding: sheets, pillowcases, duvets, and more

Mission: "Our aim is simple—to craft the very best bed linen for life from farm to finish. Sustainable. Ethical. Luxury."

LEATHER GOODS AND MISCELLANEOUS

1. Shinola

www.shinola.com

Headquarters: Detroit, MI

Manufacturing Location: Detroit, MI

Offerings: Watches, bicycles, and leather goods

Mission: "An American luxury lifestyle brand, we are dedicated to quality, craft, and creating world-class manufacturing jobs in the U.S. We believe in long-lasting products that matter."

2. Simple Wood Rings

www.simplywoodrings.com

Headquarters: Chicago, Illinois

Manufacturing Location: Chicago, Illinois

Offerings: Sustainable and Eco-Conscious wedding rings made from salvaged wood, metal, sand, and stones. Handcrafted in Chicago, Illinois, since 2005. Each handcrafted ring is treated with artisanal care.

Mission: To offer unique alternatives to the mass market while doing good for the environment. Let us tell your story.

3. Cuero and Mor

www.cueroandmor.com

Headquarters: Los Angeles, CA

Manufacturing Location: Southern Spain

Offerings: A minimalist line of handmade leather goods

Mission: "We believe there is more to the handbag industry than just slight design changes. We are introducing innovative designs and avoiding trends. We work closely with our artisans, pattern makers, and leather experts."

BONUS! A FEW OF MY FAVORITE SKINCARE & BEAUTY BRANDS

1. Dr. Alkaitis Skin Food

www.dralkaitis.com

Headquarters: Sacramento, CA

Manufacturing Location: Sacramento, CA

Offerings: Organic skin food that supports your skin's natural tasks. What goes on it, goes in it.

Description: Dr. Alkaitis only formulates with organic, biodynamic or wild-crafted herbs, plants, seeds, sea vegetables, and oils. These ingredients are of an excellent quality and sourced from the most pristine places.

2. Dr. Hauschka

www.drhauschka.com

Headquarters: Deerfield, MA

Manufacturing Location: England

Offerings: Holistic skin care created from the process invented by Rudolf Hauschka in Austria. He passed in 1969, but his brilliance lives on in his skincare namesake.

Mission: "To support the healing of humanity and the earth. Whether focusing on compost in our garden, a cultivation project in Africa, or a product formulation."

3. Josie Maran

www.josiemarancosmentics.com

Headquarters: Los Angeles, CA

Manufacturing Location: Morocco

Offerings: Luscious Argan oil-based cosmetics and skincare products

Mission: "Luxury with a conscience: we strive to create cosmetics that embody this; cosmetics that are sexy and fun, high-quality and organic, effective and good for Mother Earth. We only use pure, Fair Trade Argan oil, grown and harvested responsibly by co-ops of Moroccan women who earn a living wage."

4. Acure Organics

www.acureorganics.com

Headquarters: Fort Lauderdale, FL

Manufacturing Location: Fort Lauderdale, FL

Offerings: Organic skincare, hair, baby and wellness products

Mission: "We are a family-owned and operated company founded on sustainable principles and accessible price points to steer people away from toxic chemicals, proving that you don't need to sacrifice your health for beautiful skin and hair. We use plant- and food-based natural and organic ingredients and pure essential oils."

5. RMS Beauty

www.rmsbeauty.com

Headquarters: Charleston, SC

Manufacturing Location: Charleston, SC

Offerings: Natural beauty products made with the best organic ingredients

Mission: "We are dedicated to transforming the way women use makeup, and it's about more than simply using organic ingredients. In fact, that's only the first step in creating a product that is not only non-toxic, but that actually heals and nourishes skin. This is makeup unlike any you have seen before. Consider it skin color with mineral color."

6. John Masters Organics

www.johnmasters.com

Headquarters: New York, NY

Manufacturing Location: New York, NY

Offerings: Hair care, skin care, body care, men's, pet care, and herbology products

Mission: "We want you to feel good about looking good. We provide the finest luxury organic beauty products to customers around the world. Premium quality, earth-friendly botanical ingredients, and the ultimate in professional, salon-level results.

7. Bee Beautiful Bee

www.beebeautifulbee.com

Headquarters: CA

Manufacturing Location: Thousand Oaks, CA

Offerings: Luxury face and body oils that are infused with frequency, therapeutic bath flakes, and pink Himalayan Epsom salts.

Mission: "My passion is preserving the bee population. 10% of all proceeds go to PAN Pesticide Action Network. Our bees have been added to the endangered species list."

8. Whish Body

www.whishbody.com

Headquarters: Scottsdale, AZ

Manufacturing Location: Scottsdale, AZ

Offerings: They offer more than 70 natural body care and skincare treatment items made with luscious coconut oil, organic shea butter, rose oil, and green tea, to name a few.

Mission: "We are dedicated to the discovery of natural ingredients that enable intelligent choices for your skin."

9. True Self Organics

www.trueselforganics.com

Headquarters: Michigan, USA

Manufacturing headquarters: Michigan, USA. With the exception of a few products produced in Oregon, USA, and Canada.

Offerings: Organic skin care and hair care. Leaping bunny approved!

Mission: It is simple. We want to inspire people of the world to love themselves through, health, beauty, and self-love. In addition to using our products as part of your daily skincare regimen, self love an essential aspect of your overall health and well being. #loveyourself

INNER ALCHEMY FOR OUTER BEAUTY AND WELLNESS

It is true that what we put in our bodies will be reflected in our skin's health. Below are a few of my favorite companies for herbs, plant-based alchemy, and adaptogens. These ingredients nourish the body, elevate your wellness, and align components within your body's own chemistry so you can operate at optimum levels. These companies offer a blend of apothecaries, health foods, and medicinal remedies. Plant adaptogens enhance the body's natural response to both physical and emotional stress and assist the body in functioning optimally during stressful times. This can show externally through glowing, healthy, and supple skin and bright, clear eyes. Clarity and calmness will be reflected outward.

1. Moon Juice

www.moonjuiceshop.com

Headquarters: Los Angeles, CA

Manufacturing Location: Los Angeles, CA

Description: You can visit any one of their three locations for fresh juices, nut milks, and cosmic coffees. Their ingredients are organic, ethically sourced and wild-crafted.

Offerings: Plant-based protein powders; adaptogen dusts (Beauty Dust, Brain Dust, Sex Dust, Power Dust, Spirit Dust, and Dream Dust); pantry items such as probiotics, snacks, and a cookbook to help you make it all make sense

Mission: "Our mission is to create products for people who are interested in a new way of living—not a way where you have to erase your past, but a way fueled by excitement to help yourself live better, here and now. Moon Juice is a cosmic beacon for those seeking out beauty, wellness, and longevity."

2. Anima Mundi Apothecary

www.animamundiherbals.com

Headquarters: Long Island City, New York

Manufacturing Location: New York City

Offerings: We offer the most pristine and medicinal botanicals found in nature. Through our elixirs, superfoods, tonics, and body care, we hope to heal the mind, body, and spirit. Our ingredients are organic and wildcrafted.

Mission: To preserve the wisdom of ancient botany through indigenous wisdom, ancient formulas, and rainforest botanical treasures.

3. Sun Potion – Transformational Foods

www.sunpotion.com

Headquarters: Santa Barbara, CA

Manufacturing location: All across the world—literally!

Offerings: We offer a variety of best quality tonic herbs and superfoods. Everything from Mucuna Prurient to Pine Pollen. We also offer superfood for your skin and fluffy 100% pure shea butter.

Mission: "We are dedicated to health, happiness, and well-being through the use of medicinal plants, superfoods, and tonic herbs. We search the planet for potent, healing substances with the ability to transform consciousness and health. We work with suppliers who can meet our stringent quality standards and commitment to purity. We only source organic and wild-crafted products. We never use ingredients that have been chemically treated."

4. Super Elixir

www.welleco.com

Headquarters: Sydney Australia

Manufacturing Location: Australia

Offerings: Their first product was an all natural and whole food daily multivitamin. The Super Elixir Alkalizing formula supplement. the line has expanded to plant based protein. Calming tea and even a line for children.

Mission: The creation of Elle Macpherson and Dr. Laubscher, PhD. We believe in the importance of absorbable food based nutrients on a daily basis to maintain healthy alkaline balance. Welleco"s vision is to share their philosophies and bio live organic plant based supplements and bring a feeling of wellness to the world. We want to make it easy for people to make good choices for themselves.

Chapter 10

The Chapter of HOPE

---

*"I believe in the innate goodness in humanity.
The time for action is now. United we win,
divided we all lose." — Tracey Martin*

YES, hope is still alive, and YES, I know this world needs a healthy dose of it. When our world seems to be experiencing one tragic event after another, and the news is anything but positive, it is easy to allow it to affect our daily lives. I believe the best way to handle this is to put our time, energy, and money behind those who are doing good in the world. Not much gets accomplished when we sit in our homes and scream at the TV or computer because of all the injustices we see. We need to turn up the volume on the voices that are doing good, that are creating change, and that are looking for better ways to "BE" and "DO" in this world.

> *"Social change through industry is powerful and lasting."* — *Tracey Martin*

In the words of Mahatma Gandhi:
Keep your thoughts positive
because your thoughts become your words.
Keep your words positive
because your words become your behavior.
Keep your behavior positive
because your behavior becomes your habits.
Keep your habits positive
because your habits become your values.
Keep your values positive
because your values become your destiny.

Sometimes, we can't see a way to be a part of something or a way to help. In this book, I have listed numerous companies, brands, organizations, and individuals who can all use our support. Helping others who are already creating change can be the best place to start until your individual path becomes clear. As long as we have hope, we can move forward. The only value in looking back is so we know where we came from. We can learn from the past so that we don't repeat it. This is where we are today—let's start moving toward change for tomorrow.

One of the things I want to focus on is shining a light on those who are paving the way and doing the work to create a true shift in the fashion world. This includes revitalizing industries from bygone eras with a more evolved modern mindset and bringing life to them once again—giving a lifeline to businesses in need of CPR and maybe a little TLC, as well as giving talented individuals the opportunity to be a part of the new path of fashion. A great recipe is: opportunity + funding + talent = success.

"Do you have sight or vision? With sight, you focus on where you are. With vision, you focus on where you are going." — Tracey Martin

There are some innovative communities popping up all over the U.S. today, as well as globally. Listed below are a few of those places that give us hope to know we can do better. When brands design, develop and manufacture closer to home, they are able to leave a smaller carbon footprint and control the process in a more efficient way. It truly is a win-win for all involved. Even the customer...YOU!

These are a few fashion incubators (I am sure there are more, and I hope to tour them all) that could use our support. Incubators exist to create jobs, stimulate the local economy, add value to the community, and participate in a cultural change so that all involved can thrive. They highlight the creativity and talent of so many individuals and help present them to the world. Nurturing creative minds is the ultimate act of mentorship. I was lucky enough to tour some of these facilities and speak with their innovative founders. Below is more information on 8 such organizations. Most are non-profit organizations and are always in need of donations of monetary resources, mentors, education, and equipment. If you love fashion, think about aligning with them help to create change.

1. Arizona Apparel Foundation

Location: 132 E. 6th Street

Tempe, AZ 85282

Website: www.azapparelfoundation.org

Founded by: Sherri Barry and Angela Johnson.

Arizona Apparel Foundation is an Arizona non-profit corporation with 501(c)(3) status. The foundation's mission is to provide the knowledge and resources needed to foster Arizona's fashion industry, which can be found online at www.azapparelfoundation.org. Its vision is to support cutting-edge research and innovation in wearable technology and to build a sustainable and exciting new industry in Arizona.

FABRIC (Fashion and Business Resource Innovation Center) and Arizona Apparel Foundation (AAF) have joined forces with the City of Tempe to create a headquarters for the Arizona fashion industry. Supported by the AZ Apparel Foundation, the center will create scholarship opportunities to assist budding design entrepreneurs in scaffolding their businesses, along with offering free classes open to the public that will include everything from sewing and sketching to marketing and beyond.

2. St. Louis Fashion Incubator

Location: 1533 Washington Ave.

St. Louis, Missouri

Website: www.saintlouisfashionincubator.org
Founded by: Susan Sherman and Eric Johnson
501c3 status

Their mission is to bring fashion back to St. Louis in a BIG way by honoring their city's rich fashion history.

I had the pleasure of touring this stunningly beautiful space located in the historical fashion area of St. Louis. This building is an architecturally significant building on Washington Avenue, once known as **Shoe Street USA** for its role in manufacturing shoes, which dates back to 1878.

While touring the building, I caught up with Eric Johnson, the Executive Director. You may have heard of Eric... He is also known as New York's **Fashion Czar**. Eric comes to the role having overseen a wide range of fashion and retail initiatives. As Vice President for Arts and Fashion at the New York City Economic Development Corporation, he oversees $20 Million in fashion initiatives and has also launched numerous programs to support fashion entrepreneurs and help rebuild NYC's manufacturing industry. Here's the excerpt of my interview with Eric.

SIS: How long have you been planning the incubator?

Eric: The original idea to launch a fashion incubator in St. Louis started several years ago. I came on board as Executive Director in February 2016.

SIS: Do you offer full manufacturing capabilities in the space?

Eric: We will have sample making capabilities on the premises. A "Phase II" may include the seeding of further (full-run) manufacturing capabilities, but currently, the goal is to give our designers the ability to make prototypes onsite.

SIS: What are the services you will provide?

Eric: In addition to having access to all the manufacturing equipment onsite (e.g., industrial sewing machines, cutting tables, etc.), designers will also have access to mentorship, retail channels (e.g., pop-ups, trunk shows), and other onsite equipment (e.g., shipping, photography capabilities, etc.). Read more here.

SIS: What is the application process for the Designers in Residence Program?

Eric: We asked applicants to submit materials to give us a sense of their brand from both a business (e.g., business plan, retail accounts, etc.) and creative point of view (e.g., lookbook, social media profile, etc.). From an original group of 43 applications from 16 cities across 11 states, we went to our national advisory panel with our short list and made the final six selections.

SIS: How many designers or brands will you be working with?

Eric: The six selected brands will be located onsite. We will work with the larger STL-based designer community through programming (e.g., speakers, workshops, etc.) and tools (e.g., online directory of fashion businesses in STL, calendar of industry events, etc.).

SIS: Any unique aspects about the incubator you want to share with us?

Eric: In St. Louis (but with national connections) we feel we represent the "best of both worlds": built-in affordability of St. Louis coupled with best-in-class business building programming.

SIS: How has the community embraced you?

Eric: Given its Midwest roots, St. Louis is known for its hospitality and welcoming nature. As a native St. Louisan who chose to "come home," the reception has been wonderful.

Anyone interested in donating can contact Sarah Negrón at sarah@stlouisfashionincubator.org.

3. Chicago Fashion Incubator

Location: 111 North State Street

Chicago, Ill 60602

Website: www.chicagofashionincubator.org

Founded by: Mayor Richard M. Daley

The Chicago Fashion Incubator (CFI) is a product of Mayor Richard M. Daley's Fashion Initiative. In 2005, then Mayor Daley recognized the wide reach of Chicago's fashion industry. Realizing the significant impact fashion has on the local economy, he envisioned fashion as a driver for job creation, cultural growth, trade development, and tourism. Building on Chicago's long manufacturing heritage (two of the country's most prominent menswear brands started in the city and still make their garments there) and the city's internationally acclaimed design schools, the idea was to have a place that used the resources and opportunities available in Chicago to help aspiring local fashion designers build sustainable businesses that can compete in the global fashion industry. Thus, the Chicago Fashion Incubator was born.

The CFI is a recognized 501(c)(3) not-for-profit established in August 2008. This beautiful 2,375 sq. ft. space is located on the 11th floor of the historic Macy's State Street building and has been renovated by Beeler Construction. CFI is fully equipped with massive cutting tables, sewing machines, and pressing stations. Each designer shares a private office that is equipped with Mac computers and HP printers, all in hopes of nurturing the next big designer.

4. Fashion Incubator San Francisco (FISF)

Location: 170 O'Farrell Street

San Francisco, CA 94102

Website: www.fashionincubatorsf.org

Founded by: Macy's and Mayor Ed Lee

The mission of Fashion Incubator San Francisco, a non-profit, 501(c)(3) corporation, is to accelerate emerging apparel and accessory design businesses, while supporting the fashion industry's economic growth and job creation in the San Francisco Bay Area. Participants receive individualized mentoring from fashion industry experts and business development professionals. They help members stay current on industry trends through educational courses and free access to public programs that bring together the regional design community. They offer low-cost design studio space, a salesroom, and high-profile opportunities to showcase new lines. Fashion Incubator San

Francisco is for entrepreneurs who are serious about scaling their existing businesses.

5. Nashville Fashion Alliance
Location: 521 Gallatin Ave. Suite 10
                    Nashville, TN 37206
Website: www.nashvillefashionalliance.com
Founded by: Van Tucker in 2013

We were able to get some info from their Director of Details, Julia Dyer.

NFA was started with the help of a national Kickstarter campaign. **Nashville is the third largest fashion hub for independent designers, after NY and LA. These designers need resources, manufacturing partners, and mentoring to grow their brands.**

NFA works with a Swiss company to collect data and create a report that will show the economic impact analysis. This is needed to show the state and national level how the incubator will impact Nashville and surrounding areas so they can apply for funding and grants. NFA has relationships with universities such as Vanderbilt and is aligned with O'More School of Design.

6. Philadelphia Fashion Incubator
Location: 1300 Market Street 3rd floor
                    Philadelphia, PA 19107
Website: www.philadelphiafashionincubator.com
Founded by: Macy's Center City, City of Philadelphia, Center City District

I had the pleasure of talking with the talented **Elissa Bloom, Executive Director**. Elissa comes to the incubator with over 18 years of experience both as an entrepreneur and in the corporate sector. Having worked with Bloomingdale's and Anthropologie, she understands what it takes to create a line and get it to market successfully. Elissa is also an instructor and has taught fashion at Drexel University and Moore College of Art & Design. She even found time to launch her own accessory branded, Bloomin' Designs. Here's the excerpt of my interview with Elissa.

SIS: Can you tell me a little about PFI?

Elissa: Yes! The Philadelphia Fashion Incubator is a creative, collaborative effort between the corporate, civic, and academic communities of Philadelphia all coming together with one main mission: to support emerging fashion designers in the city and reinvigorate the once thriving fashion sector. With our founding sponsors: Macy's, Center City District, and the City of Philadelphia, along with our academic sponsors: Philadelphia University, Moore College of Art & Design, and Drexel University, we have created a dynamic, one-year residency supporting designers in scaling and growing their businesses.

Our mission is to nurture emerging fashion entrepreneurs from Philadelphia design schools and the local fashion community. By connecting them to the global fashion network and encouraging them to expand and retain their businesses in Philadelphia, the Incubator contributes to the region's economic development.

SIS: Do you have a relationship with different design schools in your state and what are the requirements to work with you?

Elissa: Yes, we do. We have partnerships with Moore College of Arts & Design, Drexel University, and Philadelphia University. Philadelphia is home to incredible fashion schools, and amazing talent is graduating from these institutions. Five years ago, there were no resources or incentives for alumni of these schools to stay in Philadelphia. PFI created our initiative with the alumni in mind who are staying in the region and starting fashion businesses.

Our ideal candidate for the residency program is a designer who has had a business up and running for six months to three years, has a cohesive collection with a point of view and value proposition, understands their positioning and target customer, and has a logo, website, and funding to support themselves and their business while in the program. We have had designers of all ages (20s–50s) and backgrounds and have worked with women's wear, men's wear, bridal, children's wear, street wear, and accessories.

7. Look Forward Project

This innovative concept is a hub on a mission to revolutionize the worlds of fashion and retail as we know it!

Location: 1 rue de bles, ZA La Montjoie - 93

      210 La Plaine Saint Denis

      Paris, France

Website: **http://www.lookforward-blog.com/**

I had the opportunity to speak with one of the **Founders, Pierre Meric.** Here's the excerpt of my interview with Pierre.

SIS: How long has Look Forward been open?

Pierre: We opened in June 2015 and incubated our first startups in September 2015. We are a part of Showroom Privé, a major e-retailer of fashion in Europe (600+ Million euros in revenue in 2015, 950 employees, profitable since its creation in 2006).

We focus on startups, not only designers, that provide new ways to produce, consume, and distribute fashion. So, we have startups focusing on not only new retail concepts, new user experiences in e-commerce, and new means of communication for fashion retailers, but also on 3D printing, wearables, etc. Our scope is quite wide, actually! Our goal is to democratize and help the digitalization of the fashion industry in France and in Europe, and to aid the Fashion Tech ecosystem in growing.

SIS: What services do you offer?

Pierre: We host projects in the Showroom Privé offices for a one-year period, with all basic facilities: Wi-Fi, post, and so on. We also provide extended coaching from the Look Forward team, our partners in banking, recruitment, UX on site, fab labs, etc., and all the Showroom Privé employees on very operational matters: SEO, recruitment, online and offline communications, media, how to build an app, how to get funds, how to be data-driven, and so on. Finally, we also set up meetings with investors (VC and BA) from our networks and access to our communication canals (PR, online) and the 1,500 brands that are customers of Showroom

Privé. The entire program is totally free for applicants; we do not take equity in startups, nor fixed fees due to the housing.

SIS: How has the fashion community embraced you since opening?

Pierre: We created strong links with fashion schools in France and the Fashion Tech community in its broad sense: other accelerators and incubators, public institutions, startups, etc. There is a strong interest in France from both the public and private sector on Fashion Tech topics, as we are a land of fashion.

8. Brooklyn Fashion and Design Accelerator

Location: 630 Flushing Ave,

Brooklyn, New York

Website: www.bkaccelerator.com

A hub for ethical fashion and design where designers transform their ideas into successful businesses. They are a new initiative launched by Pratt Institute that provides designers with the resources they need to transform their ideas into successful businesses. BF & DA brings high potential fashion designers, industrial designers, and technologists together under one roof.

Bright Futures in Historical Places

1. Hermann Oak Leather

www.hermannoakleather.com

I have been blessed to be able to visit many manufacturing facilities—some located right here in the USA. One place I toured was the Hermann Oak Leather Factory in St. Louis, Missouri. I walked the factory floor of this leather tannery that was founded in 1881. Yes! They are still doing business today and still thriving because they chose to stay connected to their heritage, integrity, and values. They tan their hides naturally with tree bark and water. They dye with vegetable dyes and only purchase hides from the meat packing facilities or stockyards. It is a sustainable, transparent, and traceable supply chain.

I have struggled with the ethics of leather in fashion for a long time. I am a non-dairy vegan, but I do have a love for fine leather goods. My personal commitment is to only purchase vintage or consignment pieces. Nothing new. In the U.S., cows, pigs, and lambs are not killed for the fashion industry. It is the insatiable appetite of meat eaters that drives this industry, and by purchasing the unwanted skins left behind, this company is remaining committed to their roots. They have created a culture within their company walls of longevity, sustainability, and integrity. I think a lot of companies could learn from them. Some of their employees have been with them for 30 years, even multi-generational family members working together.

2. The Oriole Mill

https://www.theoriolemill.com/

The Oriole Mill is located in quaint Hendersonville, NC. This beautiful mill is a true gem. I had the pleasure of meeting with the owners and walking this facility. It is forever in my heart. Here are a few words from the **Owner, Bethanne Knudson**. Some lessons for us all as well.

<u>The Oriole Mill: What We Don't Do Is as Important as What We Do</u>

The Oriole Mill is a source of beautiful, heirloom-quality fabrics and products. We think it is most important to make products that last and to make them from natural fibers. In every step of our process, we put quality first: the best quality yarn must be combined with skilled hands and expertise.

We believe that we get the best results not only by hiring the best people but also by providing them with the best equipment and the best working environment. When workers are partners, the product is better and the business runs better.

Our fabrics are as good as they look, maybe better. Our fabrics are made of 100% natural fibers. We add no chemicals, of any kind, at any stage of our manufacturing process. There is nothing to off-gas.

We perform a low-water, organic wash on some of our fabrics—not for scouring purposes, but for finishing the cloth. We do not need to scour to remove additives from our fabrics because we have not added any. The immersion and light agitation in water allows the fibers to plump and bloom. This will enhance the feel of certain fabrics, especially when using alpaca or wool yarn.

Our fabrics do not undergo any additional finishing processes. This means significantly less water and electricity is consumed, and it means the quality of the fabric is exceptional. Most finishing processes are used to make up for what the fabric lacks in terms of structural integrity or desirable hand. Superior yarns and top-quality weave constructions mean there is no shortcoming to overcome; there is no need for additional processes.

We never coat the yarn before weaving because we use extra-long staple cotton. Our cotton yarn is Pima or Egyptian Giza cotton, the best quality on earth. Our fabrics feel as good as they look, maybe better.

3. Faribault Mill
www.faribaultmill.com
"Our label is sewn into history"

This historical beauty is located in Faribault, MN, where they have been making textile products for about 150 years. Originally founded in 1865, the same year President Lincoln died and the Civil War ended, this mill is one of the last vertically integrated woolen mills left in the U.S. today. There are craftsmen working here who represent five generations before them. They use raw wool to create blankets, throws, scarves, and other beautiful, timeless accessories. The quality is uncompromising. There is irreplaceable century-old machinery standing alongside modern technology in the "new" mill that was built in

1892! This mill is a living testament to American craftsmanship. In the shop, you can purchase a beautiful blanket that looks like one that accompanied the pioneers as they were heading West. These same blankets comforted soldiers in two World Wars. A true part of American history; it is about the people!

The benefit of wool is that it is a natural and renewable resource. Scrap and even used wool can be recycled to create new blankets and throws. Unlike synthetics, wool is biodegradable. We can loosen the weave to create true summer weight woolens.

4. De La Terre Colours
www.delaterrecolours.com

Produce fully GOTS-certified natural dyes that have been specifically developed for use on a large scale and therefore optimized for fashion brands, dye houses, and textile producers. The unique all-in-one dye developed by their partners in France reduces multiple steps in the process.

Except for some tropical plants, most plants are grown by carefully selected farmers and growers in France and other European countries through exclusive partners located in the Southwest region of France. Their mission is to reintroduce the beautiful color these organic dyes produce into the world of yarn, textiles, and apparel. They do this by offering a superior, organic, and reliable product that is environmentally sustainable with full traceability from the plants to the final colors they produce.

5. California Cloth Foundry (CCF)
http://www.clothfoundry.com/#about-1

CCF makes cloth and clothes in collaboration with nature. Working closely with US farmers and ranchers, CCF procures the finest natural fibers for their fabrics and fashion. This mill creates high quality, pure and healthy soft goods while supporting fair wages and cleaner, greener manufacturing right in their backyard.

California Cloth Foundry is about trust and creating the most sustainable cloth, and clothes, possible. CCF is a grassroots company making all natural apparel and textiles that are good for people and planet alike. Within the garment industry, "sustainable" is a term in danger of losing currency. This company's understanding of sustainability starts with a transparent and well-documented local supply chain that considers the full ecological and social footprint of product development. This means that from farm to fashion, each aspect of production is labeled, barcoded, registered, inspected, and thoughtfully designed to meet the highest ecological and ethical standards. These ethos encompass not only environmentally sustainable fibers and non-toxic processes but focus on fair wages and healthy working conditions from the agricultural workers on through to the mill and factory employees. Also, there are no toxins added during yarn and cloth production or garment manufacturing. This means no harmful chemicals are released into the air or onto the skin of the supply chain partners, their employees, or you, the consumer.

"Sometimes you don't need to fight. You just need to stand strong." — Tracey Martin

These few places I mentioned are a testament to the true craftsmanship of our past fashion history and our future. These companies didn't conform or sell out. They just stood strong— not an easy task in today's *state of the fashion industry*. Hope is all around us. Sometimes we just do not see it because we are too busy complaining about things we DO NOT like, instead of supporting the things that are right in front of us. The most beautiful way to evolve is to honor the past and learn while implementing the future of positive change and influence.

"WHERE FOCUS GOES ENERGY FLOWS." — TONY ROBBINS

Start focusing on the good and see the change happen.

Some might call us movers and shakers in the sustainable fashion world; others may say we're shit disturbers, instigators or disruptors. Either way, we invite change. We make you think and ask questions. We do not believe in issuing ultimatums. Instead, we invite you through alternatives.

The following women and men are heroes for all of us who are working tirelessly to create change within the industry. It is one thing to have an ongoing conversation among manufacturers, dye houses, seamstresses, and distributors, but quite another when the voice of the masses can be heard over the white noise of the well-rehearsed sales pitches, beautiful photography, and media hype. This collective voice must demand the change we wish to see. Seek these people out, read their blogs, journals, and articles. Watch their documentaries, listen to their podcasts—they will inspire you to look past the labels on your clothing and into the storm of what can be a destructive industry. However, change is the rainbow on the horizon after the storm.

> *"You must be moved on the inside in order to take action on the outside." — Tracey Martin*

FILMS AND DOCUMENTARIES

1. Mark Angelo & Roger Williams — Documentary Filmmakers, *River Blue*

www.riverbluethemovie.eco

River Blue follows river advocate Mark Angelo on a journey through some of the most beautiful to most polluted rivers around the world. This film brings to light the dark side of the denim industry. Narrated by clean waste supporter, Jason Priestly, this groundbreaking documentary examines the destruction of our rivers, its effect on humanity, and the solutions that inspire hope for a sustainable future.

2. Andrew Morgan — Filmmaker, *True Cost*

www.truecostmovie.com

Andrew is traveling around the world to see who is making our clothing and the environmental impact it is leaving behind.

He is an internationally recognized director focused on telling stories for a better tomorrow. This documentary examines fast fashion's unadvertised sins.

3. Fisher Stevens & Leonardo DiCaprio — Filmmakers, *Before the Flood*

This film presents a riveting account of the dramatic changes in our climate and the environmental cost of our consumerism lifestyle and living without putting thought behind our actions. Time is up, and it is time to act now!

4. Jon Whelan — Filmmaker, *Stink*

Exposes chemical cancer in our everyday products. Whelan examines how dangerous, cancer causing chemicals have come to be in American products. One in two Americans will get cancer. The film takes us on a madcap journey from the retailer to the laboratory and through corporate boardrooms, down back alleys, and finally to the halls of Congress.

5. Laura Kissel and Li Zhen - filmakers, *Cotton Road*

www.cottonroadmovie.com

A brilliant documentary that follows the commodity of cotton from South Carolina farms to Chinese factories to illuminate the world and industrial processes in the global supply chain. Cotton Road uncovers the transnational movement of cotton and tells the stories of workers lives.

ORGANIZATIONS, INFLUENCERS, AND INDIVIDUALS

1. Fashion Revolution — Follow this account on Instagram. They have created a powerful platform for holding the fashion industry accountable. Pushing the concept of transparency, please take a photo with your shirt on inside out so we can see the label. Post it to their account, tag the brand, and use the hashtag #whomademyclothes. When brands are held accountable, it will let them know that we do care!

**2. Dr. Christina Dean — Founder of @getredressed
https://www.redress.com.hk/**

This amazing human founded REDRESSED, a non-profit organization and environmental NGO working to cut waste out of the fashion industry. She is also the co-founder of BYT Life, born from Redress, a line of apparel that is transforming fashion surplus into a LUXE wardrobe.

3. Greta Eagan — Eco-Fashion Stylist, @gretaegan

Sustainability expert and eco-fashion stylist at *Fashion Me Green*, Greta is a resource for aligning the world of mainstream fashion with a conscious and ethical approach.

4. Marci Zaroff — Eco-Lifestyle Visionary & Entrepreneur, @marcizaroff

Entrepreneur who coined and trademarked the term **ECO-fashion**. She is an internationally recognized ECOlifestyle visionary, authority, and educator. Marci has been instrumental in driving authenticity, environmental leadership, and social justice worldwide for more than two decades. You can follow her on Instagram and Twitter.

5. Lucy Siegle — Environmental Journalist, @lucysiegle

British journalist and writer on environmental issues. She is the author of *Green Living in the Urban Jungle*, published in 2001. Lucy is also an author and TedTalk presenter. Instagram look for the handle @theseagull

6. Sass Brown — Author, @ecofashiontalk

Author of *Eco Fashion* and *Refashioned: Cutting - edge clothing from upcycled materials*. Sass is a writer, journalist, blogger, fashion designer, researcher, and activist celebrating beauty and striving to make a difference in the world.

7. Vandana Shiva — Environmental Activist, www.navdanya.org

Indian scholar, environmental activist, and anti-globalization author. Currently based in Delhi, Shiva works hard to be the voice of the farmers working within the cotton industry in India.

To find out more about this wonderful human, visit her website.

8. Livia Firth — Founder of Eco-Age, @liviafirth

Eco-Age **(www.eco-age.com)** is an idea consultancy that powerfully aggregates global thought leaders and influencers to address the compelling issues of the fashion industry. Livia is also the founder of The Green Carpet Challenge, a dynamic platform pairing glamour and ethics to raise the profile of sustainability, ethics, and social welfare. Catapulting sustainable style into the spotlight for all to see.

9. Alden Wicker — Founder of Eco Cult, @AldenWicker

Eco Cult (www.ecocult.com) promotes sustainable and ethical fashion, non-toxic beauty, local and organic food, eco-friendly homes, and designated conscious NY events. A curious, thoughtful, utterly enthusiastic view unto NYC sustainable scene.

10. Amy Ann Cadwell — Author of *The Good Trade*, @ amyanncadwell

The Good Trade (www.thegoodtrade.com) is an online publication providing resources for ethically minded consumers through consumer guides and editorial features on social impact companies. Headquartered in Los Angeles, CA. The team at The Good Trade envisions a world where ethically minded consumers vote with their everyday purchases for a world that is sustainable and free from forced labor.

11. Kasi Martin — Fashion Writer, @ethicalwriters

Ethical fashion writer in the UK taking ethical fashion mainstream through *The Peahen* www.thepeahen.com

12. Amy Dufault — Sustainable Fashion & Lifestyle Writer and Activist, @amytropolis

Amy can be found on *Ecouterre, The Guardian,* and *Huffington Post*.

13. Safia Minney — Social Entrepreneur and Author, @ safiaminney www.safia-minney.com

She is the CEO and founder of People Tree, a pioneering sustainable and Fair Trade fashion label. Her book *Slow Fashion* is a great read for anyone looking to create change.

14. Elizabeth Cline — @elizabethcline A New York based journalist, filmmaker and public speaker. Commentator on sustainable fashion. Author of Overdressed: The Shockingly High Cost of Cheap Fashion. www.overdressedthebok.com

15. Eluxe Magazine — Editor in Chief — Chere Di Boscio
www.eluxemagazine.com **Twitter: @eluxemagazine**

Eluxe magazine is the world's first ever publication fully dedicated to sustainable luxury. They are a quarterly published paper magazine and a digital publication based in London and Paris dedicated to showcasing luxury brands that demonstrate a strong commitment to good ethics and environmental sustainability. We loved everything about this so much we requested an interview with Chere.

SIS: What is the mission of your publication Eluxe magazine as a whole?

Chere:

I aim to inform people about stuff you could never read in a traditional magazine because those publications are bound to their advertisers. So, for example, you'll never see Vogue slamming the Pink Ribbon campaign[65] for being nothing but a "corporate welfare" scam because one of their biggest advertisers is Estee Lauder. Nor will you read about how alligators and crocodiles are tortured for handbags[66] because Louis Vuitton

---

65 http://www.collective-evolution.com/2016/05/29/the-cancer-pink-ribbon-marketing-scam-thats-capitalizing-on-womens-emotions/
http://www.huffingtonpost.com/pandora-young/the-pink-ribbon-marketing_b_760696.html
66 http://www.takepart.com/article/2015/06/24/crocodile-alligator-farming-abuse-skins-hermes-fashion
http://www.dailymail.co.uk/news/article-3137714/Necks-cut-open-spines-severed-alive-just-40-000-Birkin-handbags-watchstraps-appalling-suffering-crocodiles-designer-leather-farms-exposed-undercover-video.html
https://prime.peta.org/2016/12/crocodiles-cut-open-skinned-vietnam-leather-bags

and Hermès are huge clients. Eluxe not only tells readers about unethical activities behind the scenes of fashion, and about dangerous ingredients in cosmetics and clothing dyes, but importantly also offers positive solutions to these issues.

SIS: What was the determining factor in creating your own publication?

Chere:

After having edited numerous glossy magazines from Dubai to Paris, I got fed up with having to publish nice stuff about nasty brands. I searched and searched for an ethical luxury magazine to apply to, but finding none, started my own.

SIS: What is the one burning message you want your readers and subscribers to get from your mission?

Chere:

Sustainability IS luxury. Without a thriving environment, nothing else matters. Who wants to admire something shiny and pretty whilst sitting on a garbage dump?

SIS: How would you define luxury today?

Chere:

Exactly that—sustainable. Natural. For me, any clothing brand that's been produced in a sweatshop and is full of petroleum products and harsh chemical dyes is not something I want to wear; I don't care how prestigious the label is. The same goes for skincare and cosmetics—maybe the packaging is pretty, but if it's full of chemicals that are going to give me cancer, umm...I'll pass! So luxury is, for me, beautifully made, high quality, ethically produced stuff that's ALL NATURAL.

SIS: What set you on this eco-luxury path? Anything in particular?

Chere: The blatant disregard for others and the environment that I was facing all the time working for luxury publications. For example, writing about a diamond brand I knew for a fact was selling blood diamonds. Or having to cover fur in a positive light, when I think it's horrific. Or reading Conrad Black's wife's "aspirational" words in Vogue (she literally said "My excess knows no bounds," rather proudly—just before her husband was thrown in prison for stealing from his own employee's pension funds!). Or having to write about a woman who converted to Orthodox Judaism for her wedding, then flew a whole private jet of kosher food to her wedding in St Bart's... only to discover that it was set in a non-kosher kitchen, so she *threw out all the food* and ordered a whole *new planeload* to be sent from Paris at the last minute. I was supposed to write that up as her being "a perfectionist," but she just made me sick. Promoting such products and people as "aspirational" is a form of brainwashing that tells people it's ok to be a complete tosser. It's not.

16. Conscious Chatter — Where What We Wear Matters Podcast, @awearworld

Founder Kestrel Jenkins, talks fashion, style, and sustainability on her podcast.

17. Fashion Positive C2C — @fashionpc2c

Fashion Positive C2C is the most comprehensive program in the world that guides designers and manufacturers to make products in fundamentally better ways.

18. Cradle 2 Cradle — *Remaking the way we make things*— This book was written by William McDonough with a German chemist by the name of Michael Braggart. Together they laid out a new manifesto for sustainability in all aspects of business.

ORGANIZATIONS TO WATCH, GET INVOLVED WITH, AND DONATE TO:

1. www.nrdc.org

"National Resources Defense Council works to safeguard the earth—its people, its plants and animals and the natural systems on which all life depends." This organization combines the power of more than two million members and online activists with the expertise of 500 scientists, lawyers, and policy advocates across the globe to ensure the rights of all people to the air, water, and the wild.

2. www.cleanbydesign.org

Clean by Design is an innovative program to use the buying power of multinational corporations as a lever to reduce environmental impacts of their suppliers.

3. www.apparelcoalition.org

The Sustainable Apparel Coalition is the apparel, footwear, and home textiles industry's foremost alliance for sustainable production. The Coalition's main focus is on building the Higg Index, a standardized supply chain measurement tool for all industry participants to understand the environmental, social, and labor impacts of making and selling their products and services. Their mission is to transform the apparel, footwear, and home textile industry through pioneering assessment tools, supply chain transparency, and system-wide collaboration.

4. www.earth911.com

This is a great guide for local resources including recycling centers, how to recycle, pollution prevention, efficient energy ideas, and how to protect the environment.

5. www.greenpeace.org

Greenpeace developed the Detox Fashion campaign to raise awareness about the toxic nature of the fashion industry. They have challenged some of the biggest brands to eliminate hazardous materials from their supply chain on Instagram at #detoxcatwalk.

"One's conscious evolution cannot be purchased; it must be pursued."
— Tracey Martin

I hope these resources help you! One of the biggest obstacles in the way of creating lasting change is not knowing what to do. Sustainable living is a multi-layered approach to creating true lasting change in all areas of your life. Start from where you are now. Do not worry about where you've been, only where you are going!

We believe the best is yet to come. We believe in a better fashion world and a more evolved world as a whole. Our fashion has such a profound effect on our lives and our environment. It needs to be mindfully designed, manufactured, and sold. We refuse to accept the environmental impacts of our actions; there must be change. We refuse to accept the suffering of the workers who are making our clothing. Being a rebel means you are always fighting against something. We are **REVOLUTIONARIES.** We are fighting FOR a better way. As individuals, we can create small change. As a conscious collective force, we can create a powerful, peaceful movement toward a better future.

I just have one question... What are you waiting for?

Chapter 11

Sustainable in Stilettos:

The Beyond Part — Prescription for Change

I n closing, I feel that we need to really wrap this up on a positive note. Opportunity and collaboration await us all on our journey to create sustainable living habits for ourselves, our families, and the world.

A new way of thinking—We are entering a Sustainability Revolution!

Now is the time for clarity. We are entering into a new "season" in our generation. It can be a season of incredible abundance which we can all tap into so that we can address the world's current challenges. It will enable us to move past the "lack or scarce" mindset that so many lives are built on.

"When the reason you do something changes,
you are forever changed as well."
— Tracey Martin

Throughout the book, we have talked about the fashion indus-
try, the people behind the brands, the decision makers, and the
customers. My focus now is on YOU. We truly can change this world
for the better. Nothing will bring appropriate behavior to the fore-
front like the glaring light of public scrutiny. That is where WE all
come in. We are seeking to build a better world through invitation.
Our goal is not to destroy anything or anyone. The change that we
wish to see in this world must start in the hearts and the minds of
each of us. Once we have awakened to the current situation, we
can never go backward. We can only go forward with a new found
understanding and focus on humanity as a whole.

> **"I am not calling people out; I am calling people**
> **to action." — Tracey Martin**

Fashion as a force for good must be moving forward with a
sense of action. Because negativity, corruption, fear, lack, unethical
and destructive behavior is already on the move.

The kind of change that I am speaking of is behavioral
change. It happens in stages and as an evolutionary process.
Sometimes, when we are looking to create change, we can be a
little bit clumsy in this new space. There are steps you need to
identify to make certain that you are going in the right direction.

1) Awareness
2) Identify your personal why
3) Are you willing
4) Action

5) Commitment

6) Implement change

7) Follow through

8) Accountability

9) Sharing your experience with others

10) Consistency—repeating this over and over again!

Once you have decided on a path, you must remain focused. Like I said, you might be a little clumsy at first. Be kind to yourself and forgiving. Change the self-talk in your mind to speaking inspiration and kind words to yourself. You have had a long time to develop your current habits, so it will take a little time and practice to create new ones. Remember that every decision you make will create a new "feeling." We remember feelings at the core and cellular level of who we are. Attach to the positive part of these feelings. How did you feel when you started to make a shift in your buying habits knowing that you were supporting a brand that was not only supplying you with a wonderful product but also doing good with their brand for all involved?

What does it mean to live out your values?

Let's say that you are a person of integrity. What does this really mean when applied to real life scenarios? Are you acting out of a place of abundance and progressive thinking or from a place of fear and lack? We must realize that our inner and outer worlds are connected holistically to WHO we are. It is a dynamic of our personal evolution as well as how we want to impact our world in a positive way. You have the power within you to not only shift your own habits and thinking but those of your families and your particular sphere of influence as well as your world! Once you have started this behavior in motion, create a journal on the 10 points I listed above to keep yourself accountable. To act with integrity and walk the world with your values on the outside!

> *"No problem can be solved from the same level of consciousness that created it." — Albert Einstein*

Anchor yourself in your thoughts and values. This is something I really believe in. Many years ago, I purchased a beautiful cuff that has the serenity prayer on it which reads: "God grant me the serenity to accept the things I cannot change, the courage to change the things I can and the wisdom to know the difference." I am never without this bracelet. This is what I consider my **anchor**. Whenever I am in doubt on what to do or what I believe I should do, I am reminded when I look at my bracelet. My favorite part is, "The courage to change the things I can." It will take courage at every level to stay true to the commitments you have made.

> *"So many times when we purchase food, clothing, or other items, we forget there is a person behind it." — Tracey Martin*

We all have responsibilities. Businesses have responsibilities to their employees, communities that they operate in, and customers to provide them with the highest quality on every level. This means all the way through the supply chain and to the end user. Providing people with services and products is a privilege that shouldn't be taken lightly. Remember the whole is greater than the sum of its parts. As a whole and healed industry, we can truly right the wrong that has been committed against so many and the environment. I believe good business can solve a lot of social problems and create a better world. The marketplace is where people organize, bring their creativity, test each other's values and ethics and where cultures collide and explode only to create true diversity for the benefit of all. It is a time for business to be used as an instrument for healing. To use their power and influence for good, innovation, and creativity to change the future to a more sustainable and conscious one. Business is made up of individuals. We must all evolve to the highest expression of ourselves so that we can positively impact industry at its core.

"Having the power to change something isn't always the problem. Most of the time it is having the will to do it." — Neale Donald Walsh

About the Author

Tracey L. Martin

Tracey is a Sustainable Lifestyle Leader and author. She is also a certified Transformational Life Coach, as well as a health/life and wellness advisor for more than 25 years. In addition, she is a renowned public speaker on the subject of sustainability in the fashion industry.

Tracey is a designer and founded her own line of bags by the name of Threads of Evolution. Where she uses US based artisans, plant based dyes, and a complete transparent source supply chain approach.

Tracey has maintained her mission of helping others in any way that she can. She has spoken across the country to young fashion student's about the dangers of current toxins used by today's apparel giants. As well as the educating and elevating the consciousness of todays consumers so they can make completely informed buying decisions. Having worked in the fashion industry herself for more than 19 years, with three successful brands under her belt; responsible manufacturing is nothing new to this disruptive thought leader.

Frustrated with the lack of transparency in the current "organic/low impact" dye process, Tracey decided to take matters into her own hands and partnered with the leaders in the organic dye world to create De La Terre Colours, which is GOT certified, plant based dyes, De La Terre Colours is 100% organic and truly groundbreaking in the apparel industry.

CPSIA information can be obtained
at www.ICGtesting.com
Printed in the USA
LVHW081752281218
602005LV00013B/318/P